Plantation Homes of the James River

Plantation Homes of the
JAMES RIVER

BRUCE ROBERTS

WITH EDITORIAL ASSISTANCE FROM ELIZABETH KEDASH

THE UNIVERSITY OF NORTH CAROLINA PRESS

Chapel Hill | London

Copyright © 1990 The University of North Carolina Press

The paper in this book meets the guidelines for permanence
and durability of the Committee on Production Guidelines
for Book Longevity of the Council on Library Resources.

93 92 91 90   5 4 3 2 1

Manufactured in Japan

Library of Congress Cataloging in Publication Data on page 116.

FOR NANCY LEE ROBERTS

Jamestown Island.

Contents

Preface

THE southernmost of the four Virginia rivers that flow like fingers into the palm formed by Chesapeake Bay, the James begins deep in the western part of the state. Growing ever wider, the river winds its way toward Richmond, where it tumbles and roars over the Falls, a series of rock formations which were an effective barrier to upstream navigation. East of Richmond, the portion of the river known as the Lower James continues to broaden and deepen as it flows toward Norfolk and the Atlantic, forming a deep-water highway that rises and falls with the rhythm of the ocean tides.

The Lower James dominates the landscape of this area. It is an aristocratic river—genteel and gracious in appearance but strong and powerful underneath. In the seventeenth century, the river was the only way in and out of the area, and it served as the principal highway of travel even during the eighteenth and part of the nineteenth centuries.

The land along the James is rich in history. The site of the first permanent English settlement, the area retained a prominence in national affairs until well into the nineteenth century. The list of colonial leaders from this area who played key roles in the making of the nation is an impressive one, including the Harrisons of Berkeley, the Carters of Shirley, John Tyler of Sherwood Forest, and Thomas Jefferson, who spent part of his boyhood at Tuckahoe Plantation near Richmond and frequently visited his friends at their homes along the river.

Later events bypassed the James River area. Exploitative farming practices wore out the land, and by the middle 1800s, the plantations were declining. The Civil War finished what shortsighted management had begun, and most of the estates were lost to the original families by the end of the Reconstruction period. Many fell into the hands of absentee landlords who grazed stock on the grounds or timbered the forests. The houses themselves, with few exceptions, fell into disrepair, if not ruin.

When the restoration of Williamsburg in the early decades of this century brought new attention and throngs of visitors to the area, the great houses found new owners and new prosperity. The nineteenth-century isolation of the area and the relative unprofitability of the estates now could be viewed as blessings, for the area between Williamsburg and the outskirts of Richmond had changed little over the years. Carefully restored, the plantation houses are an architectural resource and a historical treasure. As Thomas Waterman and John Burrows remarked in their 1947 publication *Domestic Colonial Architecture of Tidewater Virginia*, a visit to one of these houses "brings the past very near." With Williamsburg and the other historic sites in the Tidewater area, the plantations form a "stage set for a play that will never be enacted again."

The word "plantation" means more than just an agricultural estate. It denotes elegance and style as well as the friendliness and comfort of home. And the plantation homes along the Lower James also express a comfortable kind of aristocracy, reflecting the nature of the river as well as the status of the wealthy tobacco planters who built them.

The James River plantation homes are architectural masterpieces designed in a wide range of styles from the high Jacobean configuration of Bacon's Castle, to the formal Queen Anne symmetry of Shirley, to the Palladian mansion at Brandon. Carter's Grove has been called the most beautiful house in America, and the rich detailing of Westover's front door has been often copied.

In this book, I have focused on the major Lower James River plantations, most of which are open to the public at least some time of the year or by special arrangement with the owner. Although they share some common history, each plantation home reflects the individual characteristics of the men, women, and children who built it, lived in it, and restored it to its former glory.

For much of the information in the following chapters I owe a debt to the wealth of excellent research that has been done on these homes. But I perhaps owe more to the owners of the plantations, who graciously shared with me their own stories of events that had occurred there and the people who had lived in the mansions, for it is remembering the people and the events of their lives that makes these historic structures come alive again. And these elegant mansions were indeed homes where families lived and entertained their friends. When I photographed the dining room at Berkeley, I thought about George Washington, Thomas Jefferson, and the other eight presidents of the United States who had enjoyed meals and discussed affairs of state in that room. At Carter's Grove, I photographed the "Refusal Room," where, according to local history, both Washington and Jefferson were refused in marriage by Virginia belles. That interesting story cut history down to size for me—even men who become president have their bad days.

I fell in love with Julia Tyler, wife of President John Tyler and mistress of Sherwood Forest. She was the Jackie Kennedy of her day—young, beautiful, full of life. When she and John retired to the plantation from the White House, she had a ballroom added to the house. When I photographed that room, I could see Julia there, laughing, charming every guest, and dancing until dawn.

The name on the mailbox at Sherwood Forest today is still Tyler, and there are still Carters at Shirley and Ruffins at Evelynton. These twentieth-century descendants of the original owners are caring for the lands and homes that have been in their families for generations. To me, that is an assurance of the continuity of history, both personal and national.

There are other people who have helped save the continuity of life along the Lower James. Malcolm Jamieson has spent a lifetime restoring the house and lands at Berkeley, and Mr. and Mrs. Walter O. Major saved and restored the historic home at Belle Air. Private owners and nonprofit organizations, such as the Association for the Preservation of Virginia Antiquities, Colonial Williamsburg, the National Park Service, and the Historic Hopewell Foundation, have worked to repair and maintain other historic sites.

These people have preserved a wonderful part of America. They have made it possible for us to drive down dirt colonial roads and tree-lined drives leading to magnificent centuries-old homes where presidents can be seen as men, where history is everyday life, where we can, in a sense, discover ourselves.

One

Welcome Home, America

WELCOME HOME, America, to the James River plantations. As plantation owner Malcolm Jamieson is fond of pointing out, so many American firsts took place on the shores of the James River that this historic area is truly one of the birthplaces of the United States of America. The men, women, and children who came from Europe to the wilderness along the James in the seventeenth century established America's first permanent English settlement, produced the first manufactured goods, cultivated the first cash crop, convened this country's first democratic legislature, and observed the first thanksgiving celebration. In these and other history-making accomplishments, the James River settlers took the first steps in developing America as a new, and eventually independent, nation.

The James River story begins with the group of settlers, consisting of 105 men and boys, who boarded three small ships in England and set sail for Virginia in the late winter of 1606–7. After four storm-tossed months at sea, the *Susan Constant,* the *Godspeed,* and the *Discovery* carried the colonists between the coastal capes at the mouth of the Chesapeake Bay and into the relative safety of the broad, deep, tidal river that they named the James. The weary travelers explored the shores of the river for two weeks, searching for a suitable landing site—an inland location that the pirates and Spanish would not easily find, a place that allowed close mooring of sailing vessels and provided a healthy environment for humans and livestock.

On May 13, 1607, the leaders of the expedition chose what they considered to be the ideal area, a peninsula connected to the north bank of the river by a sandy isthmus. Having already named the river in honor of King James I of England, who had authorized the expedition, the leaders appropriately named the site Jamestown. Among the men and boys who went ashore and established this first permanent English community in the New World and the settlers who came from Europe and Africa to Jamestown in the next decade were English, Dutch, Germans, Africans, French, Belgians, Italians, Poles, Swiss, Irish, and Welsh—the forerunners of the immigrants from many nations who would build America.

The early colonists soon learned that Jamestown was not an ideal location for a settlement. The shallow, swamplike body of water between the peninsula and the mainland was infested with disease-carrying insects, the brackish waters of the James River contaminated the settlers' wells, and the town had unwittingly been built on land considered sacred by the native Americans who lived along the river. Many of the original settlers did not survive the diseases, Indian attacks, or lack of food during Jamestown's

1

An elaborate weather vane tops the cupola on the restored stable at Carter's Grove.

Scenes at Jamestown Settlement, a living-history park close to the site of Jamestown, include full-size reproductions of the *Susan Constant,* the *Godspeed,* and the *Discovery;* a church; and tobacco, planted in the style of the 1600s.

early years, but other colonists continued to come from Europe to seek their fortunes in Virginia, the first "land of opportunity" in North America.

In spite of these adversities, Jamestown grew from a quickly constructed fort surrounding rude huts into a fortified town with wooden houses, a main street, and a church. As more and more settlers arrived, homes and farms spread to the land outside the walls of the fort. Except for the "pitch and tar" swamp in the middle of the area, homesteads eventually covered almost the entire peninsula, which was two and a half miles long and about one mile across at its widest.

The Jamestown colonists not only overcame the incredible difficulties of surviving in a wilderness but also started America's first business enterprises, manufacturing items for their own use as well as products to sell in Europe. Soon after their arrival in the New World, the settlers began making fishing nets, pottery, tools, bricks, and clapboards. By 1609 they had produced the first glass made in North America.

As the colonists became increasingly self-sufficient and less dependent on supplies and support from Europe, their desire for self-government grew. On July 30, 1619, over a year before the Pilgrims' ship landed in New England, the leaders of Jamestown convened the House of Burgesses, the first representative legislative body in this country.

Many of the earliest Jamestown settlers came to America hoping to find in the soil along the James River the fabled gold and mineral riches that the Spanish explorers had found in Mexico and South America. Virginia did not provide quick and easy fortunes, however. The "gold" in Virginia was in tobacco, a crop that required skill, patience, and hard physical labor to produce.

John Rolfe, a tobacco-smoking Englishman who came to Jamestown, experimented with Indian tobacco that grew along the James River and developed a sweet-leafed variety that sold well in England and other parts of Europe. Rolfe's successful experiment gave the Virginia colonists their first major cash crop, and by 1618 settlers had moved westward from Jamestown, planting tobacco in the fertile soil along both shores of the river.

Some of the colonists who settled the banks of the James River had been granted huge tracts of land by the Virginia Company of London, the group of financiers that had the rights to settle the new continent. In order to encourage more people to go to America, the company gave land grants to men who had the funds to transport people to Virginia. The Virginia Company used the word "plantation" to refer to the group of people who were to settle permanently on a tract of land, but the term soon came to mean the land itself rather than the people who lived on it. "Hundred" was another term used to refer to some of the larger James River plantations, perhaps because one hundred settlers was the ideal number of people for a plantation or because the first "division" of land made by the Virginia Company for "ancient" planters was one hundred acres.

The James River plantations were separate communities, with each plantation owner responsible for the well-being and safety of the people who lived on his land. In order to retain the title to his plantation, the owner was required to erect a modest dwelling and farm a portion of the land. As long as the owner paid the annual quitrents, he had the right to sell his plantation or pass it on to his heirs. Ownership of the plantations along the James River changed hands often, depending on the success or failure of the tobacco crops grown on the land.

In the next hundred years, some of the river plantations developed into large-scale agricultural and commercial operations. In addition to tobacco, crops were grown to feed the plantation community. Extra wheat and ground meal and even hard biscuits were sold to the crews of the ships that docked at the plantation wharves. Artisans made clothes for the community from tanned hides, cotton, and wool and built the necessary buildings.

5

The Jamestown settlers replaced their sod church with a brick structure. The tower ruins
still stand today at Jamestown National Historic Site.

The plantation sawmill produced planks and clapboards for the community's needs as well as milled lumber to ship to England. Along with being centers of business, the James River plantations served as centers of hospitality and social life during America's early days.

One of the first plantations to be settled outside of Jamestown was established by John Martin, who had come to Virginia in 1607. Martin disagreed with Lord Delaware, the governor of Jamestown, and was banished from the settlement in the spring of 1610. Taking a few of his supporters with him, Martin moved across the James River to a site on the south shore. Martin's settlement flourished, and in 1616 he returned to England, taking a full cargo of products from the plantation.

While in London, Martin obtained an official grant and a charter for his plantation, which he named Brandon. Unfortunately, a fire in the late 1620s destroyed most of the buildings at Brandon and sent him into bankruptcy. He died, almost penniless, in 1632.

In 1610, about the same time that John Martin took his followers across the James River to establish Brandon Plantation, Lord Delaware sent a group of men led by his nephew Henry West to look for gold in the remote area along the north shore of the river west of Jamestown. Even though the explorers did not find gold, the governor ordered them to spend the winter in the area. The men built small houses and a wall to protect their temporary settlement. However, an arrow shot at random over the wall by an Indian killed Henry West. To make surveillance of the area easier, the men erected a watchtower, which they named West Tower in memory of their leader.

The following year, Lord Delaware's brother, Sir Francis West, arrived at the site and claimed it for a new community of his own. West's huge tract of land was called West and Shirley Hundred. Although Indian uprisings interrupted efforts to colonize this area, eventually Westover, Shirley, Evelynton, Berkeley Hundred, and a number of smaller plantations were established in this vicinity.

In 1618 the Virginia Company of London granted a group of Englishmen a charter to establish Berkeley Hundred, a new plantation to be located on part of the land already claimed by Francis West. The Berkeley colonists left England on September 16, 1619. When they reached Jamestown two and a half months later, they met with Sir George Yeardley, who had become governor after Lord Delaware's death. Yeardley placed the new plantation on land next to West and Shirley Hundred. The thirty-nine Berkeley colonists came ashore at the plantation site on December 4, 1619, and following written orders from England, they immediately held a service of thanksgiving for their safe arrival. This first American thanksgiving continued to be observed annually at Berkeley Hundred.

While Berkeley and other plantations on the north shore of the James were developing, civilization was also spreading westward along the south shore of the river. Around 1617, Sir George Yeardley began cultivating one thousand acres of land upriver from John Martin's Brandon Plantation. When Yeardley became governor and captain-general of Virginia in 1618, he was granted a charter for his plantation, which he named Flowerdew Hundred to honor the family of his wife, Temperance Flowerdew. Because Yeardley preferred to live in Jamestown, he appointed an overseer to manage the plantation, which by 1619 was producing substantial tobacco crops. In 1621, Yeardley had North America's first windmill built on his land to grind corn and wheat grown at Flowerdew and neighboring plantations.

The colonists were not the only people living along the James River during the seventeenth century. About thirty tribes of Indians that had been forcibly united under the powerful chief Powhatan fished, hunted, farmed, and built their lodgings in the

Tidewater area. Although some of the Indians who lived along the James occasionally attacked individuals or groups of settlers, others made friends with the colonists and traded corn, game, and furs for trinkets, tools, and guns. A number of the plantations employed Indians as hunters, and a few of the colonists who deserted the English settlements were accepted by Powhatan and allowed to live in his village. For the most part, the Indians allowed the communities to develop, expecting the high mortality rate from diseases, accidents, and natural causes to keep the settler population low.

As more and more colonists arrived in the New World and claimed tracts of land along the James, however, many of the Indian tribes relocated their villages farther away from the English settlements. Beginning about 1614, the colonists rapidly expanded their control of the land, planting tobacco on fields that the Indians had already cleared. Alarmed by the increasing number of colonists and their determination to establish permanent communities, the Indians carefully planned and skillfully executed an uprising to eliminate the settlers.

During the winter of 1621, the Indians were especially friendly and won the trust of the colonists. When the Indians started drifting into the plantation communities early in the morning on Good Friday, March 22, 1622, the settlers were not alarmed. Then, in an extremely well-coordinated breakfast-hour assault, the Indians surprised and attacked the settlers on some twenty-five plantations, completely wiping out some of them. By the end of the day about 350 men, women, and children—almost one-third of the settler population—had been massacred. The Indians also slaughtered plantation livestock, set fire to the buildings, and destroyed the stores of corn.

Jamestown had also been scheduled for destruction, but when groups of Indians drifted idly toward the town that Good Friday morning, they found the people of Jamestown armed with muskets, ready for the attack. They had been warned of the uprising by Richard Pace, a planter on the north shore mainland near Jamestown who had treated an Indian convert like a son. This Indian, named Chanco, had been ordered to kill Pace in the morning assault, but after struggling with his conscience throughout the night before the surprise attack, the Indian revealed the whole plan. Pace rowed across the backwater to Jamestown in time to prepare the settlers.

The survivors from the destroyed plantations were ordered to retreat to Jamestown for protection and food. In May 1622 the colonists were ready to retaliate, but by that time most of the Indians had disappeared from the area, abandoning their ancient homelands. The colonists quickly drove off the few remaining small groups of natives.

As the threat of future attacks diminished, the surviving landowners petitioned the Council of Jamestown for permission to return to their plantations. Some of the landowners invested much time and money in attempts to revive their plantations, while others simply gave up and eventually sold their lands. At the plantations where there had been no survivors, the land either passed on to heirs in England or was granted to new owners by the governor.

Within a few years, despite the devastating massacre and the difficulties of rebuilding, the James River plantations were once again producing extremely profitable crops of tobacco. The settlers quickly suppressed a second major Indian uprising on March 18, 1644, and forced the Indians to cede their rights to all the land along the James below the upstream falls. By 1650 conditions were relatively peaceful and stable, and even though the mortality rate was still higher than it was in England, new colonists coming to the river communities had a better chance of living a normal life span.

Bacon's Castle.

Oil lamps at Smith's Fort.

Although the majority of the settlers owned isolated small farmsteads, a number of the landowners accumulated huge tracts of farmland and managed large work forces, which included indentured servants and, by 1700, an increasing number of Negro slaves. The indentured servants earned their freedom after working for the plantation owner for a specified number of years, but the slaves, part of the communities along the James since 1619 when the first group of twenty was brought to Jamestown aboard a Dutch ship, were bought outright and remained the property of the plantation owner for life. Because the slaves provided long-term, relatively less expensive manpower, they became the primary labor force on the larger plantations.

In the late 1600s, many of the smaller farmers sold their lands to wealthier neighbors as fortunes were made and lost in the cultivation and sale of tobacco. Eventually, a few landowners controlled most of the tobacco land and money, and classes of society began to emerge, with the owners of the large plantations and their families forming an aristocratic upper class. The upper class provided the strong leadership, and the Negro slaves and the middle- and lower-class small farmers and skilled freemen provided the manpower and skills that allowed civilization in Virginia to rapidly expand and strengthen. During the last half of the seventeenth century, the plantation system along the James flourished, and the money earned from tobacco financed an opulent life-style for the upper-class families in the eighteenth and early nineteenth centuries.

By the early 1700s, many of the larger James River plantations were in the hands of the second- and third-generation descendants of the original landowners. From childhood, they had been trained to be astute businessmen, knowledgeable farmers, capable lay doctors and veterinarians, and effective supervisors. By the time they inherited their estates, these men were able to skillfully manage thousands of acres of land and the numerous indentured servants and Negro slaves who provided the manpower needed for the successful operation of the plantations. Even though the owners had trusted overseers to help with the day-to-day management of the estate, the master of the plantation would personally inspect his fields, warehouses, stock barns, the wharf and sawmill, and the outbuildings where wool was carded, hides were tanned, barrels were made, and food was prepared. In addition, the owner did the plantation paperwork, keeping detailed records and writing business letters.

Along with their practical training in plantation management, these eighteenth-century owners had been taught at least the basics of reading, writing, and arithmetic. Some of them were sent to Europe for schooling, and many were well-educated individuals who enjoyed reading, writing, music, and the arts. They entertained their friends lavishly with banquets, balls, horse races, and other festivities. And they built fine mansions that reflected their affluence and prominence in society.

One of the first mansions to be built along the James River was the grand three-story house at Shirley Plantation. Work on the structure began in the 1720s, and the mansion, which took at least fifteen years to complete, was an architectural masterpiece.

Elizabeth Hill, mistress of the mansion, had inherited the estate soon after her marriage to John Carter, the son of Robert "King" Carter, who was considered to be the wealthiest man in colonial Virginia. Throughout the eighteenth century, the Hills and Carters who lived at Shirley entertained many of the prominent families and government leaders of Virginia, including the Harrisons, the Byrds, the Randolphs, the Lees, George Washington, and Thomas Jefferson. Bonds of friendship and marriage brought these influential colonial Americans together often at the James River plantation homes.

9

The Harrison family lived in the stately Georgian-style mansion at Berkeley Hundred, the next plantation downriver from Shirley. Benjamin Harrison IV built the three-story home in 1726 when he married Anne Carter, the daughter of King Carter.

The Harrisons and the other owners of large plantations built their homes not only to shelter their own families and numerous house servants but also to accommodate the innumerable guests that were part of plantation life. Like the other riverfront mansions, the Berkeley house had two front doors for guests to use—*the* front door that faced the James River, a primary route of travel in colonial days, and at the opposite side of the house, a door that faced the one-and-a-half-mile-long private driveway off the public road.

The Harrisons, like the Hills and Carters next door at Shirley, were leaders in Virginia government and entertained many important colonial Americans, including George Washington and Thomas Jefferson.

The Byrd family lived at Westover Plantation, the estate on the east side of Berkeley Hundred. William Byrd II built the elegant mansion at Westover in the 1730s. Byrd, a handsome, colorful man known as the "Black Swan," was in his fifties when he started work on his home, and he spared no expense in constructing the three-story mansion designed with simple, classic lines and graceful proportions.

Byrd's son and heir, William Byrd III, was master of Westover Plantation in the latter half of the eighteenth century when the colonists from New England southward became increasingly resentful of England's interference in American affairs. Byrd and most of the colonial leaders of Virginia were reluctant to rebel against England, for even though they owned vast amounts of land in America, they still considered England their homeland. Many of them had been sent to England for schooling, and their English heritage was deeply inbred in them. But the seeds of independence and self-government had been planted in America by the early settlers at Jamestown, and the ideals of representative democratic government were an integral part of Virginia's history from the convening of the first House of Burgesses in 1619.

Convinced of the need for American independence, Benjamin Harrison V, Charles Carter, George Washington, Thomas Jefferson, and other Virginians played leading roles in the events leading up to the Revolution. Many of the James River plantation owners served as members of the First and Second Continental Congresses held in Philadelphia. Jefferson, who spent part of his childhood at Tuckahoe Plantation just west of Richmond, was the primary author of the Declaration of Independence, and his friend Benjamin Harrison V of Berkeley presided over the Continental Congress debates that culminated in the acceptance of the Declaration. Harrison was among the signers of that document, and Washington, another friend, assumed command of the American military forces during the Revolution.

Although most of the battles took place outside Virginia, the James River area did not escape involvement in the events of the war. Shirley Plantation served as a supply center for the Continental army, and because the plantation was located between the British camp at City Point and General Lafayette's camp at Malvern Hill, Shirley was used as a surveillance post twice by both sides.

Berkeley Hundred and some of the other river plantations were plundered by British troops until the British were defeated by the combined American and French troops in the last major campaign of the war, which ended on October 19, 1781, at Yorktown, about twenty miles east of Jamestown. George Washington declared an end to the hostilities when the British and Americans signed a provisional treaty in November 1782. The Ameri-

Tuckahoe Plantation, the boyhood home of Thomas Jefferson near Richmond, preserves one of the most complete sets of existing colonial plantation dependencies, including these original slave quarters.

Flemish-bond brickwork at Evelynton.

One of the dependencies at Shirley Plantation houses the original kitchen, where meals were prepared for the family as well as guests, including George Washington and Thomas Jefferson.

can colonies officially became independent when the final treaty was signed on September 3, 1783.

Virginians, including the families of the James River plantations, continued to play important roles in the government of the new nation. Four of the first five presidents came from Virginia, and Virginians Thomas Jefferson and James Madison were instrumental in shaping the structure of the federal government. In the early days of the United States, George Washington, Thomas Jefferson, and other national leaders continued to come to the river plantations to visit their friends and discuss affairs of state. Each of the nation's first ten presidents enjoyed the hospitality of the Harrisons at Berkeley Hundred.

In 1841 the Harrison family provided the ninth president of the United States, William Henry Harrison, who had fought the Indians in the Northwest Territory and earned the nickname "Old Tippecanoe." Although he made his home in Ohio, Harrison returned to the room where he was born at Berkeley to write his inaugural address.

The tenth president, John Tyler, was born near Berkeley at Charles City. Tyler was Harrison's vice-president and became president when Harrison died a few weeks after his inauguration. After completing his term as president, Tyler retired to Sherwood Forest, a plantation located east of Westover Plantation on the James River.

By the time Tyler moved into his plantation home in 1845, many of the James River estates were in a state of decline. Two hundred years of tobacco crops had worn out the land, and other crops could not produce the enormous incomes needed to maintain the grand mansions and huge estates. Many of the owners had incurred insurmountable debts, and with the events of the Civil War and the subsequent loss of slave labor, the golden age of the James River plantations came to a close.

The James River area was a focal point of conflict during the Civil War. In 1861 Virginia seceded from the Union, and Richmond became the capital of the Confederacy. Virginia was the major battleground for the ensuing four years of fighting.

The river plantations suffered heavy damage during the war. Evelynton Plantation, originally part of the Westover estate and purchased by Edmund Ruffin, Jr., in 1847, was the site of intense skirmishes in the summer of 1862. The existing house was plundered and almost totally destroyed and the plantation lands laid to waste.

Berkeley Hundred served as headquarters for General George McClellan and the Federal Army of the Potomac from July 2 to August 16, 1862. Throughout the summer, Union men, animals, guns, and wagons trampled the plantation fields and the quarter-mile between the mansion and the river, and Union transports and gunboats controlled the James River near the plantation wharves.

Shirley Plantation served as a shelter for Union soldiers wounded in one of the bloodiest campaigns of the war, McClellan's Peninsula Campaign to capture Richmond. For days during the summer of 1862, the Hill Carter family provided food, bandages, and other supplies for the injured men until ships arrived at the plantation wharves to transport the wounded to Union hospitals. The soldiers who died were buried at the plantation.

During the Petersburg Campaign of 1864, Shirley was again in the midst of the fighting. The plantation family managed to raise enough food to survive and to salvage some of their belongings from their house, which was plundered by the soldiers. On April 9, 1865, Hill Carter's cousin, Confederate General Robert E. Lee, surrendered to General Ulysses S. Grant at Appomattox Courthouse, Virginia.

While Shirley and some of the other plantations survived the destruction of the war, Evelynton and countless other large and small estates did not. Many of the plantation families fled their homes as the Confederate and Union troops advanced, and when the families returned to their estates at the end of the war, they found only burned-out shells of buildings and desolated farmlands.

Lacking the money and labor force to rebuild their homes and lands, many of the plantation families abandoned their estates. A number of the once-grand mansions along the James River were left to decay until the early 1900s, when they were inherited or purchased by owners who recognized their historic value and began to restore them.

Shirley Plantation is now in the hands of the ninth and tenth generations of the Hills and Carters, its founding families. Hill Carter, the current owner, was raised in the plantation house, and he and his wife, Helle, have brought up their own children in the mansion, which they opened to the public in 1952. They consider living on the estate a personal adventure in history that they want to share with others.

Berkeley Hundred, abandoned for seventy-five years, was purchased for timberland in 1905 by John Jamieson, a New York Scotsman who had served as a drummer boy with McClellan's troops that were stationed at the plantation in 1862. When John's son, Malcolm, acquired the property, he began the long process of restoring the mansion and the grounds. Malcolm and his son use some of the plantation land for a large commercial nursery that produces their famous Berkeley boxwoods and raise grain, hay, sheep, and timber on the remaining acres. Like the Hill Carter family at neighboring Shirley Plantation, Malcolm and his family want people to visit their estate, and they opened their plantation to the public in 1938.

Payne and Harrison Tyler express the same respect for history at their home, Sherwood Forest. The Tylers acquired the estate from family members in 1975 and worked two and a half years to restore the manor house, which had been heavily damaged during the Civil War.

Belle Air Plantation, close to Charles City just west of Sherwood Forest, is the site of one of the oldest existing dwellings in English America. The main part of the structure was probably built about 1650 by Thomas Stegge II, a wealthy settler who left the bulk of his wealth to his nephew William Byrd I, whose son built the mansion at Westover. Periodic repairs and an eighteenth-century addition gave the house an early Georgian appearance. Belle Air was abandoned in the early twentieth century, and it was not until the estate was purchased for its farmland in 1947 that the value of the house was recognized. In the 1950s the new owners began the process of repairing and restoring the historic structure.

The current owners of nearby Westover Plantation continue to maintain that estate, with its 150-year-old tulip poplars that shelter the impressive Georgian mansion. The building that in the restored house forms the east wing, and which once held the four thousand volumes of William Byrd II's impressive library, burned during the Civil War. The house was repaired and remodeled about 1900.

In the 1930s, John Augustine Ruffin, Jr., began restoring Evelynton Plantation, which had been almost totally destroyed during the Civil War. Architect W. Duncan Lee designed the new mansion, incorporating ideas from Shirley, Westover, and other historic plantation homes.

Across the James River from Evelynton and the other north-shore plantations are several historic estates that have also been restored and opened to the public. Weston Manor, located west of Hopewell, overlooks the Appomattox River. The late-Georgian clapboard house was built in the 1700s as a wedding gift for a member of the Eppes family. The colonial wharf has been reconstructed, and the house is furnished with period pieces.

Appomattox Manor, located where the Appomattox River joins the James at Hopewell, also belonged to the Eppes family. In 1635, Francis Eppes received a grant of seventeen hundred acres and brought his three sons and thirty servants from England to the plantation. In the mid-1700s, Eppes's grandson built the fine manor house that is now open to the public. General Ulysses S. Grant headquartered his Union troops at Appomattox Plantation during the Civil War and used a T-shaped cabin on the grounds for his field office.

Downriver from Appomattox Manor is Flowerdew Hundred, where a film and exhibit tell the story of almost four centuries of English civilization at the site. Although excavations and historical documents have revealed that a 1620 manor house and at least eleven other buildings protected by a four-thousand-foot-long palisade once stood there, the only existing structures are an eighteenth-century-style windmill erected by the cur-

Carter's Grove as evening approaches.

A cannon at Malvern Hill, part of Richmond National Battlefield Park, marks the site of the last battle in the Seven Days Battle of 1862. After the battle, the Union troops retreated to Berkeley Hundred and used the plantation mansion as a field hospital.

Maple trees once again line the entry road on the restored grounds of Bacon's Castle.

rent owner in the 1970s and an antebellum schoolhouse. The plantation land has yielded a wealth of archaeological artifacts, some dating back to 9000 B.C.

On the south shore of the James River east of Flowerdew Hundred is John Martin's Brandon Plantation. Ownership of this estate changed hands several times after Martin's death in 1632. Although Nathaniel Harrison purchased the land in 1720, his son was the first family member to live at the estate. The existing house is thought to have been designed by Thomas Jefferson, one of the groomsmen in Nathaniel Harrison II's wedding. The house bears the scars of two wars—marks of bullets fired at it from a British ship on the James River during the Revolution and damage by the soldiers who occupied the estate during the Civil War. Today, there are twelve families living at the plantation, which produces substantial crops of corn, soybeans, wheat, and barley.

Further east on the south shore of the river, almost directly across from Jamestown, is Smith's Fort Plantation, the site of a fort that Captain John Smith ordered to be built in 1609 as a haven in case the Indians attacked Jamestown. In 1614 the powerful Indian chief Powhatan gave this land to John Rolfe as a wedding gift when Rolfe married Pocahontas, Powhatan's daughter. Thomas Rolfe, their son, inherited the land in 1635 and later sold it to Thomas Warren. In 1653, Warren built a brick house, known as the Fifty Foot House, which has disappeared. The existing 1760 colonial Virginia country house, which was restored by John D. Rockefeller in 1935, was probably built by a descendant of Thomas Gray, who owned a large adjoining plantation.

The most impressive manor house on the south shore of the Lower James River is Bacon's Castle. Claimed to be the oldest brick house in English America, the 1665 structure was built by Arthur Allen in the shape of a cross with three clustered Jacobean chimneys at either end. In 1676, Nathaniel Bacon occupied Allen's house and used it as a fortress for three months during his rebellion against the leaders of Jamestown. The Association for the Preservation of Virginia Antiquities purchased the estate in 1973 and has restored the house as well as the extensive gardens.

Chippokes Plantation, near Bacon's Castle on the south shore of the James, is owned and managed by the Commonwealth of Virginia. Farmed continuously since 1621, Chippokes is believed to be one of the oldest working plantations in North America. This estate, like others, has changed ownership many times and was the site of several homes. The late-eighteenth-century house that now stands vacant near the river was probably built on the foundations of earlier structures. In 1918, Victor Stewart and his wife purchased the estate and began restoring the 1854 manor house, which had suffered many years of abuse. Mrs. Stewart gave the property to the Commonwealth of Virginia in 1967 as a memorial to her husband.

Carter's Grove is on the north side of the James River close to Williamsburg. Robert "King" Carter, the wealthiest man in colonial Virginia, started construction on the mansion in 1750. It was home to members of the Carter family until 1838, when it was sold outside the family. The estate fell into disrepair, and ownership changed hands many times until Mr. and Mrs. Archibald M. McCrea purchased the property in 1927. With the help of architect W. Duncan Lee and other professionals, the McCreas restored the mansion to a Colonial Revival showplace. Now owned and maintained by Colonial Williamsburg, this architectural masterpiece is beautifully furnished in the style of the Virginia gentry and is open to the public.

Today's owners of the plantation homes, many of which have been designated state and national historic sites, invite visitors to come to the James River area and relive almost four hundred years of America's history.

17

Two

Shirley Plantation

SHIRLEY, ONE OF THE oldest plantations in Virginia, boasts a unique historic continuity. Mentioned in documents dated as early as 1611, this tract of land was inhabited by 1613 and was already producing tobacco to be exported to England by 1619. Colonel Edward Hill purchased the plantation in 1653 and seven years later completed building a house on the estate that has been in the hands of the Hill-Carter family ever since.

Colonel Hill, who has been described as a "feisty, two-fisted, swashbuckling Englishman," exemplified the daring and ambition needed to succeed in the New World. He actively pursued careers in politics, the military, real estate, and commerce and firmly established his family's holdings in the untamed wilderness on the north shore of the James River. In the centuries to come, Colonel Hill's descendants would continue to build and maintain Shirley with the same determination and dedication to hard work exhibited by the founder of the family estate.

Edward Hill II followed his father's lead in colonial affairs and served as captain of the militia, sheriff of Charles City County, surveyor of highways, and a justice on the county court. After his father's death in 1663, Edward became master of Shirley's extensive landholdings. He expanded Shirley's commercial enterprises by completing a tannery that his father had started, building a tavern that not only provided room and board for travelers but also served as the county jail, and increasing farm production by raising cattle, hogs, sheep, and poultry as well as planting corn, wheat, barley, oats, and tobacco.

Both the Hill family and Shirley suffered a major setback in the summer of 1676 when Nathaniel Bacon and his followers stormed the plantation in their rebellion against the Jamestown governor and Loyalists, such as Edward Hill. Bacon and his men plundered the plantation home, destroyed the livestock and crops, and beat and held captive Edward, his pregnant wife, and their children. Bacon's death from dysentery in October and the arrival of military reinforcements from England in January ended the unsuccessful rebellion, and the Hill family returned to Shirley and began rebuilding their home and farmlands.

By the time Edward Hill III became master of Shirley at the turn of the eighteenth century, the plantation was again flourishing. Like his father and grandfather, this Edward also actively participated in colonial affairs by serving in the militia, in the House of Burgesses, on the board of governors of the College of William and Mary, as the officer in charge of clearing outgoing and incoming ships on the upper portion of the Lower James River, and as a member of the vestry of Westover Church. The family estate prospered under Edward's management, and the Hills lived well and entertained often at Shirley Plantation.

The dovecote, used to raise squab, is one of Shirley's elaborately built eighteenth-century dependencies.

Hill Carter is the ninth-generation owner of Shirley Plantation.

One of the door keys rests in its original lock at Shirley Plantation.

An old trunk sits in a corner of one of the dependencies.

The family cat naps in the parlor, oblivious to its historic surroundings.

Family records show that Edward Hill III had at least two children—Edward IV, who died about the age of 16, and Elizabeth, who inherited the estate. The existing grand mansion at Shirley was built for Elizabeth in the early 1700s. It is not known for certain whether Edward had the house built for his daughter or if Elizabeth's husband had it built shortly after their wedding. Elizabeth's marriage to John Carter, son of Robert "King" Carter, united the Hills with the very wealthy and influential Carter family. In the years that followed, the Hill-Carter family of Shirley Plantation became famous for its gracious and lavish hospitality.

When Elizabeth and John's son Charles Carter inherited the estate about 1769, he enlarged and renovated the house and dependencies to accommodate his large family—Charles fathered twenty-three children, some of whom died in infancy. He was master of Shirley during the events leading up to the American Revolution. Although he felt a sense of loyalty to England, once war was inevitable, Charles actively supported the rebellion. During the Revolution, he fought in the militia, and Shirley Plantation served as a supply center for the Continental army and as a reconnaissance post for both the British and American forces.

Despite the Revolution and the changes brought about by America's independence, Shirley Plantation continued to prosper. In the late 1700s, Charles purchased many elegant furnishings for his home, including numerous pieces of English silver engraved with the family crest and dining room armchairs carved with the head of the dog on the Carter family coat of arms.

Charles's daughter Anne and Revolutionary War hero "Light-Horse Harry" Lee were married at Shirley in 1793. Their son Robert E. Lee attended school classes held in one of the dependencies at Shirley.

Charles's son Robert Hill Carter chose to study medicine rather than become master of Shirley. Robert, a widower, left his children with their grandparents and traveled to Paris for postgraduate medical studies. When Robert died in 1804, Charles designated Robert's young son Hill Carter as heir of the estate when he came of age.

Hill Carter's uncles managed the estate poorly in the first years of the new century, but when Hill took possession of Shirley in 1816, he set about to restore the plantation. With determination and skill, he replaced worn-out farm equipment, motivated his workers to greater productivity, and experimented with new crops and advanced farming methods. Under Hill's strong management, the estate once again began to prosper. Unfortunately the events leading up to the Civil War and the war itself brought hard times to Shirley and the other James River plantations.

In the four years of war, Shirley was in the thick of the fighting during the Peninsula Campaign and the struggle to control nearby Richmond, the capital of the Confederacy. During the last week of June 1862, Shirley served as a field hospital for the thousands of Union soldiers wounded in the bloody six-day Battle of Malvern Hill. In her memoirs, Louise Carter, wife of Hill's son Robert Randolph Carter, recounts details of life at Shirley during that time. She tells of the injured soldiers lying on the lawn around the house and up and down the riverbank, and she describes how for days the family provided soup, bread, water, and cloth for bandages, until enough ships arrived to transport the survivors to hospitals. Union General George B. McClellan expressed his deep appreciation for the southern family's help and provided the Carters with safe-conduct passes and other courtesies.

After the war, the Carters once again picked up the pieces of their lives and possessions and rebuilt their family estate. Robert Randolph Carter became master of Shirley in

Shirley has been a working plantation for more than three hundred years.
Old farm equipment is displayed in one of the original barns.

The crested silver teapot, brought from England, reflects the prosperity enjoyed by the Hill-Carter family at Shirley during the eighteenth and early nineteenth centuries. The beautiful chandelier hangs in the dining room, where many prominent guests enjoyed Shirley's gracious hospitality.

1866 and faced the task of working the plantation without the help of slave labor. Following his father's lead, Robert purchased labor-saving equipment and experimented with new farming methods to increase the yields with less physical labor. Robert's dedication and determination paid off, and Shirley continued to be a working plantation.

Although Robert had no sons to inherit the plantation, he did have a widowed daughter who took a lively interest in managing the estate. When Robert died in 1888, Alice Carter Bransford became the mistress of Shirley. Alice's strong commitment to her family's estate led her to be personally involved in every aspect of the plantation, from feeding the mules to supervising the farm workers to mending harnesses. Alice earned a reputation for being the best farmer on the James River.

In 1917, Alice's cousin Charles Hill Carter, who lived at High Hill across the road from Shirley, took over the management of the plantation farmlands. In 1921, Alice's sister Marion and her husband came to live with Alice at Shirley. Alice died in 1925, and three years later, Charles and his family moved to Shirley to help the recently widowed Marion.

With no direct descendants to inherit the estate, Marion, in accordance with her father's will, chose an heir from among her grandfather's descendants. She chose Charles's son Charles Hill Carter, Jr., better known as Hill Carter.

Marion chose wisely, for Hill had grown up in the plantation home and had helped his father manage the estate for many years. Shirley's new master, the ninth generation to live on the plantation, embodies the Hill-Carter family's love and pride in Shirley as well as the determination and dedication to hard work exhibited by his forefathers.

Almost 350 years ago, Edward Hill I was granted land in Virginia "for personal

The walnut staircase, which rises three full stories with no visible support, floats upward from the entrance hall.

Anne Hill Carter and "Light-Horse Harry" Lee, parents of Robert E. Lee, exchanged marriage vows in this room at Shirley.

adventure," a concept that Hill and his wife, Helle, have kept alive. Hill opened Shirley to the public in 1942. He married Helle in 1960, and their children have grown up sharing their historic home with thousands of visitors each year. As it has for the past 250 years, the 3-1/2-foot-tall pineapple finial in the center of the mansion roof still symbolizes the warm hospitality offered by the Hill-Carter family at Shirley Plantation.

The road off State Road 5 leading to the plantation is lined with fields of soybeans, corn, wheat, and other crops. Even though they live in a National Historic Landmark, Hill and his family consider themselves to be farmers, and they continue to work the eight hundred acres of the existing estate.

Stately Lombardy poplars guard the quarter-mile-long dirt road that approaches the mansion. A number of the original eighteenth-century dependencies form a Queen Anne–style forecourt, the only one of its kind in the United States. These plantation dependencies, which were elaborately built of brick laid in the Flemish-bond pattern, include a two-story kitchen, the laundry that was converted into a schoolroom for Robert E. Lee and other young family members, a dovecote, a smokehouse, a stable, and two barns, one with an icehouse beneath it.

Shirley's mansion and its dependencies are architectural treasures. Like the dependencies, the house is also built of bricks laid in the Flemish-bond style. The rubbed brick used in the arches above the windows matches that in the dependencies. The three-story home is topped with a unique mansard roof.

Only the four rooms on the first floor of the house are open to the public—the family

Sketches of early family members hang above the table, which displays several pieces of the Hill-Carter family's crested English silver.

uses the remaining floors for living areas. One of the main doors of the house faces the forecourt, but *the* front door of the mansion is on the opposite side of the home, facing the James River, which was the primary highway during the early eighteenth century when the home was built. The mansion is close enough to the shore that the river can be seen from the front porch. The front door and the main door on the back side of the house are directly opposite each other and are so carefully aligned that if both doors are opened at the spring and autumn equinoxes, the sun setting across the James is framed in the doorways.

Superb paneling and elegant carved woodwork fill the inside of the mansion. A graceful walnut staircase, which rises the full three stories without visible support, dominates the entrance hall. The flooring is heart pine in random widths, and the walls are painted a pale, pinkish-rose color that is believed to be similar to the original interior color.

In 1793 the formal living room on the first floor was the scene of the wedding of "Light-Horse Harry" Lee and Anne Hill Carter, the parents of Robert E. Lee. Throughout the eighteenth, nineteenth, and twentieth centuries, the Hills and Carters entertained many prominent Americans at Shirley, including George Washington, Thomas Jefferson, John Tyler, Teddy Roosevelt, and John Rockefeller. Family portraits and furniture, crested English silver, and memorabilia give visitors an intimate look into the past at this home, which is now lived in by the ninth and tenth generations of the founding family.

27

Three

Berkeley Hundred

A<small>T 8 O'CLOCK</small> on Thursday morning, September 16, 1619, Captain John Woodlief and the thirty-eight carefully selected men who would settle Berkeley Hundred set sail from London aboard the *Margaret*, a forty-seven-ton ship. After two and a half stormy months at sea, the settlers sailed into Hampton Roads and after a brief stop at Jamestown, proceeded up the James River to the plantation site. Following written orders from Berkeley's financial backers in London that the day of the settlers' arrival "be yearly and perpetually kept holy," the men came ashore and immediately held a service of thanksgiving for their safe journey. This first American thanksgiving celebration, held more than a year before the Pilgrims landed in New England, marks the beginning of Berkeley Hundred's well-documented story, which is highlighted by many historic events.

Under the leadership of Captain Woodlief, a seasoned colonist who had survived the early years of settlement at Jamestown, Berkeley's original colonists planted Indian corn, wheat, garden crops, and tobacco, the main cash crop. They also raised cattle and hogs and sold fish, clapboards, and timber for shipbuilding. The colonists also searched for iron ore on the plantation lands and experimented with grapevines for the production of wine and mulberry trees for the cultivation of silkworms.

Despite the success of the plantation's first year, the colonists needed to have a supply ship sent to Berkeley from London in 1620. Blaming Woodlief for not making the colonists self-sufficient, Berkeley's financiers replaced Woodlief with George Thorpe, an Englishman especially interested in converting the Indians to Christianity. According to local history, when Thorpe arrived at Berkeley and learned that the settlers had to drink water instead of spirits, he immediately set about to rectify the situation. Thorpe experimented with Indian corn grown on the plantation and produced America's first whiskey. The settlers and Indians who sampled Thorpe's brew declared that it was much better than the English variety.

In the next two years, more settlers, including women and children, came from England to the plantation. Even though the death rate was high at Berkeley and the other fledgling settlements along the James River, the plantation developed into a firmly established community. The Indian Massacre of 1622, however, abruptly ended life at Berkeley Hundred.

Early in the morning on Good Friday, March 22, 1622, the Indians surprised the settlers and completely destroyed the buildings, crops, livestock, and supplies at Berkeley. Although the historical records are not complete, documents show that none of the colonists remained at Berkeley after the Indian attack. Most of the settlers were either killed at the plantation or died later of wounds. One twelve-year-old boy may have been captured

by the Indians, and several other settlers may have escaped, but none of the survivors returned to Berkeley to resettle the plantation.

In the years following the massacre, new groups of colonists came to Berkeley, and ownership of the plantation changed hands several times until the Harrison family bought the property in 1691. Benjamin Harrison III, who was the attorney general and treasurer of the Virginia colony, moved to the plantation in the mid-1690s. By 1695, he had established one of America's earliest commercial shipyards at Harrison's Landing, the deep-water landing site on Berkeley's three-mile-long riverfront.

Harrison's son and heir, Benjamin Harrison IV, was born in the small house that stood on the property. Like his father and most of the other James River plantation owners, this fourth-generation Harrison was active in colonial affairs, serving as the county sheriff and as a member of the House of Burgesses. Benjamin united his influential family with the powerful Carter family when he married Anne, the daughter of Robert "King" Carter, who was considered to be the wealthiest man in colonial Virginia. Befitting his social position and affluence, Benjamin built the impressive Georgian mansion at Berkeley in 1726.

Benjamin Harrison V, who was born in the mansion soon after it was completed, followed in his forefathers' footsteps as a colonial leader and held many public offices during his lifetime, including three terms as governor of Virginia. This Harrison served as a member of the Continental Congresses, signed the Declaration of Independence, and actively participated in the American Revolution. During the war, British troops under Benedict Arnold raided Berkeley Hundred, killed the livestock, stole a number of the slaves, and burned the Harrisons' personal belongings, family portraits, and the mansion's damask draperies and other furnishings in a spectacular bonfire.

Despite the destruction caused by the Revolution, the plantation and the Harrisons survived and continued to play a primary role in America's development as an independent nation. The family frequently entertained George Washington and other prominent leaders at Berkeley. All of the first ten presidents enjoyed Berkeley's famous hospitality, including family member William Henry Harrison, who became the ninth president.

William Henry Harrison was born at Berkeley in 1773. The third son of Benjamin Harrison V, William left Berkeley to pursue a military career. He served as the governor of the Northwest Territory and earned the nickname "Old Tippecanoe" for his success in subduing the Indians. When William was elected president in 1841, he returned to the room where he was born to write his inaugural address. William's grandson, Benjamin Harrison, was elected the twenty-third president in 1888, making Berkeley the ancestral home of two presidents.

In the 1840s Berkeley and many of the other James River plantations fell into a state of decline, and a few years after William Henry Harrison wrote his presidential address at Berkeley, the Harrison family lost ownership of the plantation. Worn-out land and insurmountable debts put Berkeley in the hands of the Bank of the United States. The estate was purchased by a succession of owners, each of whom tried unsuccessfully to restore the productivity of the land.

The last of the transient owners packed their belongings, locked the doors of the mansion, and left Berkeley Hundred when the Union and Confederate forces began fighting their way along the James River toward Richmond during the Civil War. Berkeley and many of the neighboring plantations sustained heavy damage in numerous bloody battles during the four years of fighting.

From July 2 to August 16, 1862, Union General George McClellan headquartered his

Union General Dan Butterfield composed "Taps" while stationed at Berkeley during the Civil War. When his bugler, Oliver Wilcox Norton, first played the new "lights out" call, Confederate buglers camped on the other side of the James picked up the haunting tune and played it back across the water. Fighting during the American Revolution and the Civil War left visible scars on many of the plantation homes. A Civil War cannonball remains lodged in the wall of one of Berkeley's dependencies.

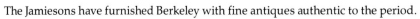

The Jamiesons have furnished Berkeley with fine antiques authentic to the period.

Federal Army of the Potomac at Berkeley Hundred. President Abraham Lincoln visited the plantation at least twice during that time to confer with McClellan and to review the 140,000 soldiers encamped in the fields and the quarter-mile-wide landscaped area between the mansion and the river. Throughout the summer, Union transports and gunboats docked at Berkeley's old wharf, the historic Harrison's Landing, as they guarded the riverfront.

During that summer at Berkeley, one of McClellan's generals, Dan Butterfield, helped his bugler, Oliver Wilcox Norton, compose a new tune for the evening "lights out" call. When Norton played the melancholy notes of "Taps" for Butterfield's soldiers, the officers of other divisions heard it and had their buglers repeat the call. Confederate soldiers camped on the south shore of the James also heard the bugle call and picked up the haunting melody, echoing it back across the river. Soon "Taps" was played not only at twilight but also at military funerals, including the funeral of Confederate General Thomas Jonathan "Stonewall" Jackson. Eventually "Taps" became an official bugle call of the U.S. Army.

In his retreat after the Seven Days Battle around Richmond, McClellan used the abandoned mansion at Berkeley as a field hospital. Rain fell steadily as the Union troops tramped across Berkeley's fields and carried the wounded into the mansion. In a desperate attempt to dry out the walls of the abandoned house and to provide some warmth for the injured, the soldiers built fires in the mansion's fireplaces, burning whatever they could find, including the remaining furniture.

The Union soldiers were the last people to occupy Berkeley Hundred until John Jamieson, a Scotsman from New York, bought the mansion and the surrounding fourteen hundred acres in 1905. Jamieson, who had served as a drummer boy with McClellan's troops stationed at Berkeley, purchased the estate for timberland. One of his sons, Malcolm, grew to love Berkeley and dreamed of resurrecting this proud ghost of the past and restoring it to its former grandeur.

After his father's death, Malcolm bought out the other twelve heirs and set about to revitalize Berkeley's farmlands and to repair the mansion. With determination and an incredible amount of hard work, Malcolm has made Berkeley Hundred a working plantation that yields more per acre now than ever before and has renewed the beauty of the early Georgian home.

Malcolm and his family opened Berkeley to the public in 1938, and they enthusiastically welcome visitors to share in the history of their 370-year-old plantation. A historic colonial dirt road off State 5 links Berkeley with the modern world. Timber, farm crops, sheep, and cattle fill the acres along the road and around the mansion. The Jamiesons use part of the land as a commercial nursery where they raise their famous Berkeley boxwoods.

Malcolm has planted more than twelve hundred crepe myrtles, tulip poplars, magnolias, black locusts, and other trees to replace the ones destroyed during the Civil War. He has also restored the five landscaped terraces and the manicured lawn between the mansion and the James River. Where Union soldiers once set up camp, a formal boxwood garden, a rose garden, and the ladies' winter garden once again flourish. Numerous quail, eagles, wild turkeys, ducks, and many species of songbirds nest on the plantation lands.

Just making the mansion livable again was a massive undertaking. All of the locks were broken, all of the windows were knocked out, sheep had been penned in the basement, the first floor had been used for a grainary, pigs had been fed out of the dining room, the outside bricks had been covered with red barn paint, there was no central

Malcolm Jamieson has spent his lifetime restoring the grandeur and productivity of Berkeley Hundred.

36

Dogwoods and hundreds of other trees and shrubs fill the restored gardens at Berkeley.

Benjamin Harrison IV and his wife, Anne, placed this datestone, inscribed with their initials, over a side door when they built the mansion in 1726.

In this painting on display at Berkeley, the three-story plantation house rises above the slave cabins.

heating or cooling system, and none of the furnishings remained in the three-story structure. Despite the state of disrepair, Malcolm moved into the mansion when he acquired the estate, and in the years he has lived at Berkeley, he has continued to work to restore and improve the beautiful home.

Malcolm, who considers himself to be a "caretaker of history," starts tours of Berkeley Hundred in the basement of the mansion, where the original hand-hewn joists are visible. He invites visitors to watch a ten-minute audiovisual presentation about Berkeley and the other early settlements along the James River and to view historical paintings and exhibits.

Visitors tour the entrance hall, the great room, the dining room, and the master's study on the first floor of the mansion—the Jamiesons use the two upper floors of the home as living quarters. The great room has two sections and can be used as one large room or two smaller rooms. The handsome Adam woodwork, hand-carved by slaves, was added in 1790 at the suggestion of Thomas Jefferson. A small butler's pantry opens off the dining room. The master's study was used as a spare bedroom and a family room. Malcolm's wife, Grace, researched the interior of the mansion and chose colors thought to be close to the original paint. The Jamiesons have furnished the rooms with beautiful eighteenth-century antiques.

The mansion is flanked by two of the original dependencies, both of which were enlarged and remodeled about 1800. One of the buildings was the plantation kitchen, and the other served as bachelor's quarters. In the eighteenth and early nineteenth centuries, numerous other buildings, housing the plantation's skilled workers and slaves, surrounded the mansion.

Malcolm Jamieson has dedicated his life to restoring and maintaining Berkeley Hundred, which has been designated a National and State Historic Landmark. It is with great pride and personal commitment that Malcolm says to Berkeley's visitors, "Welcome home, America."

The gazebo on the front lawn at Berkeley provides a view of the sun setting over the James.

Belle Air.

Sherwood Forest.

Four

Belle Air Plantation and Sherwood Forest

I F T H E P E O P L E who purchased Belle Air Plantation for its farmland in 1947 had not been curious about the history of the deserted frame house that stood on the grounds, this unique seventeenth-century architectural treasure might have been torn down or left to decay. An eighteenth-century addition and three hundred years of repairs had given the exterior an early Georgian appearance, masking the original seventeenth-century features. Although previous brief research had failed to reveal any information about the home before 1800, the new owners undertook more extensive research and learned that the main part of the house dated to the middle 1600s.

Judging from the overall quality of the construction, the ornamental carving on the framework, and the beautiful Jacobean staircase, architectural historians were able to determine that the home was built by one of the wealthier settlers of early Virginia. However, it is not known for sure who built the original main portion of the manor, which has been added on to through the centuries. Two prosperous men owned the property in the last half of the 1600s. In 1653, Colonel Thomas Stegge II inherited his father's merchant business, ships, and the seventeen-hundred-acre plantation on the James River. Historical documents show that Stegge brought his family from London and completed a home on the plantation land by 1655. Lieutenant Colonel Daniel Clarke purchased the property in 1662, and documents dated 1665 refer to Clarke's plantation home, which perhaps was the manor built by Stegge. Clarke's descendants named the plantation Belle Air in the late eighteenth century.

Hamlin Willcox purchased the plantation in 1800, and although the house was deserted in the 1920s, Belle Air remained in the Willcox family until 1945. In the 1950s the current owner, Mrs. Walter O. Major, and her late husband carefully repaired the plantation manor, which is one of the few surviving examples of the modest frame homes built during the first century of America's history.

The 1-1/2-story house was built of wood. The huge, hand-hewn, heart-pine timbers were skillfully carved and left partially exposed inside the house to serve as decorative woodwork as well as structural framework. A beautiful hand-carved balustrade highlights the home's original Jacobean staircase, one of the finest of its kind in America. White plaster walls complement the rich, warm colors of the woodwork and the heart-pine mantels and floors. Period furnishings enhance the simple, inviting feeling of this three-hundred-year-old National and State Historic Landmark. By appointment, visitors may tour the home, smokehouse, well house, old kitchen, and grounds, which include a formal herb garden. The home may also be toured during Historic Garden Week.

This plantation bell still rings at Sherwood Forest.

Julia and John Tyler added the sixty-eight-foot-long ballroom to the west wing of the mansion.

46

Many of the windows at Sherwood Forest retain their original lead glass.

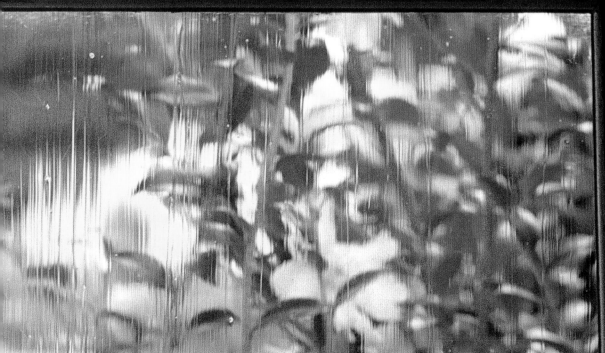

President John Tyler and his wife, Julia, renovated and enlarged the existing mansion at Sherwood Forest. In the dining room, architect Minard Lafever added the door on the left for balance—even though the door goes nowhere. During the Civil War, Union soldiers pried off the door ornaments throughout the house; they took the ornaments from the door on the left but overlooked the matching set on the other door.

An unusual design marks this eighteenth-century dependency used to store dairy products. The curved roof, made of plaster of paris, helps the cooler air close to the brick floor flow upward.

Payne Tyler enjoys sharing the history of Sherwood Forest with visitors.

The side wings of Sherwood Forest extend outward in a straight line from the center section of the house. Reaching a total of one hundred yards (the length of a football field), Sherwood Forest is the longest wood frame house in the United States.

At the nearby Sherwood Forest plantation, beautiful grounds shelter a three-hundred-foot-long manor home, the longest frame house in America. Measuring the length of a football field, the house appears to be even longer because of the linear placement of its original dependencies—the manor, smokehouse, wine house, necessary house, and milk house form one continuous progression.

The original part of the house, built in the first quarter of the eighteenth century, was only half the size of the existing structure. John Tyler, who became the tenth president of the United States in 1841, renovated and doubled its size in the 1840s. The estate had been previously owned by his friend William Henry Harrison, who was the ninth president—making Sherwood Forest one of only two homes in America owned by two presidents.

Tyler had reluctantly agreed to be Harrison's vice-presidential running mate and unexpectedly became president when Harrison died just one month after his inauguration. Tyler's first wife died shortly after he took office, and during his last year as president, he married Julia Gardiner, who was only twenty-four years old when she became first lady. The Tylers retired to Tyler's plantation, then known as Walnut Grove, when he completed his term in 1845. Tyler renamed the estate Sherwood Forest because during the time he was president, he had been called Robin Hood by Henry Clay for promoting legislation that enacted some of the first national social programs to help America's poor.

Because the Tylers had personally paid the majority of the costs of decorating and furnishing the White House during their tenancy, they brought many of the furnishings with them to their plantation home. They entertained many prominent people at Sherwood Forest, and the mansion's sixty-eight-foot-long ballroom often held festive galas, where the Tylers and their guests danced the Virginia reel and Tyler entertained with his original violin compositions.

Gold leaf architectural embellishments, designed by the New York architect Minard Lafever, decorate the manor's drawing room. The spacious home, which includes two- and three-story sections, has seven full sets of stairs, with an appropriate name for each set, including the "Fall Down Stairs" in the gray room and the "Suicide Stairs" in the sitting room.

Even though John Tyler was seventy-two years old when Virginia seceded from the Union during the Civil War, he allowed himself to be elected as a member of the Confederate Congress. However, he died in Richmond in 1862, before the congress was convened.

Like the other James River plantation homes, Sherwood Forest stood in the thick of the fighting during the Civil War. Union generals McClellan, Butterfield, and Butler and their troops camped on the plantation grounds.

Today, John Tyler's descendants still live at Sherwood Forest and farm the plantation's sixteen hundred acres. Payne and Harrison Tyler acquired the estate from family members in 1975 and spent two and a half years restoring this uniquely American mansion, which has been designated a National and State Historic Landmark. The Tylers offer tours of their home only by special arrangement, but they open the estate's twelve-acre grounds to the public daily.

More than eighty varieties of trees fill the land around the home. John Tyler brought many of them from the National Botanical Gardens in Washington, D.C. Behind the house stands a ginkgo tree that Commodore Matthew Calbraith Perry presented to Tyler after one of his trips to the Orient.

Westover.

Evelynton.

Five

Westover and Evelynton Plantations

ONE OF THE first areas that America's early settlers explored outside of Jamestown was the land that later became Westover, Evelynton, and several other plantations. In 1610, Lord Delaware, the first governor of Jamestown, sent a group of men to search for gold in the upstream wilderness along the north shore of the James River. The band of explorers built a small walled settlement on the tract and erected a watchtower, which they named West Tower.

Before 1622, Lord Delaware's brother, Sir Francis West, patented the tract of land for a new community. Although historic records indicate that West lived at the plantation site, the devastating Indian Massacre of 1622 interrupted permanent settlement of the area for the next fifteen years. In 1637, Thomas Paulett repatented the tract, giving it the name Westover. Theodoric Bland purchased the property and existing buildings in 1666 and then sold the plantation to William Byrd I in 1688.

William, however, bought the plantation only as an investment and continued to live at the trading post he had established at the upstream falls of the James. When William's son, William Byrd II, completed his education in England and returned to Virginia in the late 1720s, he found his father's remote outpost too far from civilization, and he decided to settle at Westover instead. About 1730, William Byrd II built the impressive three-story brick mansion there that commands admiration even today.

Byrd, a colorful man known as the "Black Swan," spared no expense in building and furnishing his beautifully proportioned, classic Georgian home. Ornately carved plaster ceilings, hand-carved decorative woodwork, richly paneled rooms, and an unusual black mantelpiece add touches of elegance to the interior of the mansion. The elaborate doorway that graces the main entrance to the home has often been copied and adapted to other buildings.

Two smaller brick buildings originally flanked the mansion, one at each end in line with the main home. One building was the kitchen, and the other held Byrd's library, which included more than four thousand volumes written in English, French, Latin, Hebrew, and Greek. As Byrd's extensive writings indicate, he undoubtedly spent many hours in his literary sanctuary filling the pages of his diary, which he recorded daily for years, and preparing his numerous well-written papers and letters.

Byrd's son and heir, William Byrd III, incurred numerous personal debts during the late 1700s, and in 1814 the family was forced to sell the estate. Westover changed hands many times during the nineteenth century, until it was purchased by the Fisher family, whose descendants have made Westover their home for four generations.

The building that housed William Byrd II's famous library was destroyed during the Civil War, and when it was rebuilt about 1900, both of the smaller buildings were con-

The beautifully detailed, hand-carved doorway at Westover is probably the most copied doorway in America.

Eighteenth-century wrought-iron gates guard the land entrance to Westover.

A fireplace warmed the "necessary"
in winter.

55

nected to the main body of the mansion. The Fisher family offers tours of their home only during Historic Garden Week each spring, but invites the public to explore Westover's beautiful grounds and historic dependencies daily year-round.

Three wrought-iron gates protect the entrances to the estate. The intricate design of the pediment over the main gate includes William Byrd II's initials. The large, sculptured lead eagles perched atop the ten-foot-high gateposts are a play on the name "Byrd." Topping the supporting columns of the wrought-iron fence are unusual stone finials cut to resemble an acorn for perseverance, a pineapple for hospitality, a Greek Key to the World for knowledge, a horn of plenty, a beehive for industry, and an urn of flowers for beauty.

Towering 150-year-old tulip poplars shelter the mansion, and an ancient boxwood hedge encloses the lawn that sweeps down to the shore of the James. Just east of the mansion are the icehouse and a small building that contains a dry well with underground

The front lawn of Westover sweeps down to meet the James.

Built in the 1730s, Westover exemplifies the stately air and graceful proportions of Georgian architecture.

passageways leading from the house to the river, escape tunnels in case the plantation was attacked.

A brick fence surrounds the mansion's formal boxwood garden, which was restored about 1900. The handsome marble obelisk at the center of the garden marks the grave of William Byrd II, who built the home and planned the landscaping. Byrd wrote his own epitaph, providing an intimate glimpse into how he viewed himself, and perhaps how he wanted to be remembered: " . . . [the] well-bred Gentleman and polite Companion, the splendid Occonomist and prudent Father of a Family . . . the constant Enemy of all exhorbitant Power and hearty Friend of the Liberties of his County. . . ."

Historic Westover Church originally stood close to the estate's garden. The church served the families of Westover, Berkeley, Shirley, and adjoining plantations, and many of the parishioners stayed after the Sunday services to visit the Byrds at their nearby mansion. According to local legend, Mrs. William Byrd II became weary of entertaining so many guests each Sunday, and the Byrds had the church building dismantled and moved along a specially built half-mile-long causeway across Herring Creek to its present site. Then they had the causeway destroyed so that would-be Sunday visitors would have to make a four-mile trip by carriage or horseback to reach the Westover mansion.

The Revolutionary War and America's independence from England ended services at this Anglican church, and the building where George Washington, Thomas Jefferson, William Henry Harrison, John Tyler, and other prominent colonial Americans had worshiped stood empty for many years. In 1830 missionaries from England came to Virginia to promote the Episcopal church, the American branch of the Anglican community. Westover Church, which had been used as a barn for forty years, was restored in 1867 and has been continually used for worship services since that time.

One of the young women of the early eighteenth century who dreamed of being married in Westover Church was William Byrd II's daughter Evelyn. Her dreams were not to be fulfilled, however, because Byrd would not allow her to marry her sweetheart, the rakish grandson of the Earl of Peterborough. Evelyn refused to marry anyone else and died, perhaps of a broken heart, before she reached the age of thirty. Evelyn is buried near the original site of Westover Church, and her ghost is said to haunt Westover as well as Evelynton Plantation, the tract of land Byrd separated from Westover and gave to his wife in honor of Evelyn.

The Byrd family sold Evelynton, and ownership of the plantation changed hands several times before Edmund Ruffin, Jr., purchased the estate's original 860 acres at an auction in 1847. The owner's father, Edmund Ruffin, Sr., is perhaps best known as the intense Southerner who fired the first shot of the Civil War at Fort Sumter in April 1861. However, the senior Ruffin was also a renowned agriculturist who developed new fertilization methods to restore the productivity of the tobacco-exhausted lands along the James River. Innovative farming techniques made Evelynton one of the more prosperous plantations along the north shore of the James in the mid-1800s, but as with so many other Virginia estates, the events of the Civil War all but destroyed the property.

During the Peninsula Campaign in the summer of 1862, Union soldiers under General George McClellan marched through the area. Throughout the summer, Confederate generals J. E. B. Stuart and James Longstreet fought numerous fierce skirmishes with the Union troops to control the strategic high ridge of land at Evelynton. The soldiers plun-

George Washington, Thomas Jefferson, William Henry Harrison, John Tyler, and other prominent colonial Americans worshiped in historic Westover Church. The restored building is still used for services.

A double-gate entry guards the
final approach to Evelynton.

Elaborately carved woodwork enhances the interiors at Evelynton.

62

Elizabeth M. Ruffin, holding daughter
Elizabeth Harrison Ruffin, stands
beneath the portrait of Edmund
Saunders Ruffin in the living room
at Evelynton.

In the 1930s, the Ruffin family commissioned renowned architect W. Duncan Lee to design Evelynton's new Georgian Revival mansion, which incorporates details from the other plantation homes
along the James. The view from the living room into the main hallway and the dining room beyond
gives an impressive display of the architectural detailing of the home.

The gardens at Evelynton.

Old silver and candlelight grace the dining room table of the Ruffin family home.

A portrait of Robert E. Lee guards the stairway at Evelynton.

dered and burned the plantation home and dependencies, spread salt on the fields, and girdled the trees on the plantation land.

Although Evelynton remained in the hands of the Ruffin family, it was not until the 1930s that the plantation was restored. John Augustine Ruffin, Jr., the great-great-grandson of Edmund Ruffin, and his wife, Mary Ball Saunders, a prominent Richmond heiress, commissioned architect W. Duncan Lee to design a Georgian Revival house to be erected on the foundation of the original home. Lee borrowed the best architectural elements from Westover, Shirley, Carter's Grove, and other historic plantation homes in planning the new Evelynton mansion, which was built with 250-year-old bricks. The Ruffins have furnished their family home with American and European antiques, many of them family heirlooms. The family welcomes visitors to tour the home and grounds of Evelynton every day except Thanksgiving, Christmas, and New Year's Day.

American and European antiques fill the beautifully detailed rooms of Evelynton.

Appomattox Manor.

66

Weston Manor.

Six

Appomattox Manor, Weston Manor, and Flowerdew Hundred

B EFORE selecting Jamestown as the most suitable location for their settlement, the colonists who came from England to America in May 1607 explored the banks of the James River for two weeks. Their explorations took them as far upstream as the junction of the Appomattox and James rivers, an area inhabited by the Appomatuck Indians. Even though the colonists rejected this location for their first town, early records indicate that after Jamestown was settled, some of them sailed back upstream and were entertained by Opusoquoinuske, queen of the Appomatucks.

As the early colonists began to settle lands outside of Jamestown, a group of men under the leadership of Sir George Yeardley built a palisade around a huge tract of land on the south shore of the James that included the area surrounding the mouth of the Appomattox River. Sir Thomas Gates, the governor of Jamestown, named the tract Bermuda Hundred, in memory of the time he had spent shipwrecked in Bermuda while en route to Virginia. The natives destroyed this settlement in the 1622 massacre, and even later, when the threat of Indian attacks had diminished, few people returned to resettle this plantation community. Although the low-lying land was extremely fertile, periodic flooding made it less attractive than other areas. All traces of the early settlements at Bermuda Hundred have disappeared.

In 1635, Francis Eppes patented seventeen hundred acres of the land at the mouth of the Appomattox River. Eppes, a wealthy Englishman who had come to Virginia about 1617 and had served as a burgess in the first Assembly in 1619 and as a member of the Council in 1635, received an additional 650 acres when he brought his three sons and thirty servants from England to his plantation.

Eppes named his plantation Hopewell Farm to commemorate the ship that had carried him from England to Jamestown, and he called his plantation home Eppington. Eppes's grandson tore down Eppington in the mid-1700s and replaced it with Appomattox Manor, the fine house that stands on the property today. Thomas Jefferson's daughter Mary married Eppes's great-grandson and lived in the manor house for several years before she died of cancer at age twenty-five.

Several dependencies were built on the property in the 1800s, and the east wing was added to the manor house in 1840. Like the other plantation homes along the James River, Appomattox Manor suffered in the wars that raged through the Virginia Tidewater. During the Revolutionary War, British soldiers under General Benedict Arnold marched

67

Appomattox Manor sits alone on the point of land where the Appomattox River joins the James. Twentieth-century urban development crowds the adjacent riverbanks (*following page*).

through the estate, trampling the gardens and fields. From June 1864 until April 1865, General Ulysses S. Grant made the plantation his headquarters, first using a tent erected on the east lawn and later a T-shaped cabin. President Abraham Lincoln used the drawing room of Appomattox Manor as his office when he visited the plantation to confer with Grant. During the siege of Petersburg, most of Grant's troops and supplies traveled up the James River and came ashore at nearby City Point.

Appomattox Manor remained in the Eppes family until 1979 when the U.S. National Park Service purchased it to become part of the City Point unit of the Petersburg National Military Park. The twenty-three-room manor home, Grant's headquarters cabin, and the grounds are now open to the public daily.

On a bluff overlooking Appomattox River just west of Appomattox Manor stands Weston Manor, said to have been built as a wedding gift for a member of the Eppes family in the 1700s. The property surrounding the home, which is called Western Manor in some historical documents, is probably part of the land patented by Francis Eppes in 1635. The property remained in the Eppes-Gilliam family until it was purchased by Patrick Dolin in 1869. In 1962 the Dolin family sold the estate to the Broyhill family. Recognizing the historic value of the eighteenth-century plantation home, Raymond Broyhill donated Weston Manor and one acre of the surrounding grounds to the city of Hopewell with the condition that the house be restored and used as a cultural center. The Historic Hopewell Foundation was formed in 1970, and with the assistance of grants from the Department of the Interior, private contributions, and community effort, the foundation is working to restore this National and State Historic Landmark.

While this late-Georgian, three-story, white frame house is not one of the most elegant colonial homes, it is an outstanding example of the fine handcrafted buildings constructed during that time. The house, which has not been structurally altered since it was built, retains almost all of its original interior woodwork, molded weatherboards, and window sashes. Each of the rooms includes a fireplace, and the heart-pine floorboards show evidence of the wooden pegs used when the floor was laid. Many of the windowpanes are the original glass, filled with small air pockets and other irregularities. A graceful spiral staircase, with its polished mahogany railing and hand-carved concave paneling lining the circular side, rises at the end of the twenty-five-foot-long entrance hall.

During the Civil War, a cannonball shot from a gunboat on the river below the house lodged in the dining room ceiling. Union officers, including General Philip Sheridan, used the house during the siege of Petersburg and scratched their names in one of the windowpanes as evidence of their occupation. Mathew Brady, one of America's most famous late-nineteenth-century photographers, accompanied the Union army during the Battle of Petersburg and photographed Weston while it was occupied by Union troops.

In accordance with Raymond Broyhill's stipulation, Weston Manor now serves as a museum and cultural center for the city of Hopewell. The house is furnished with period pieces, and the grounds and colonial wharf have been restored. The estate is open to the public during Historic Garden Week and at other times by appointment.

Downriver from Hopewell is Flowerdew Hundred, site of North America's first windmill. Sir George Yeardley began cultivating one thousand acres of this fertile tract of land around 1617. When he became governor and captain-general of Virginia in 1618, he received a charter for his plantation, which he named after his wife, Temperance Flowerdew. In 1621, Yeardley had a windmill erected at the plantation to grind corn and wheat grown at Flowerdew and other plantations.

Flowerdew Hundred was one of only seven settlements to survive the devastating Indian Massacre of 1622, and when Abraham Peirsey, a wealthy merchant, purchased the

General Ulysses S. Grant used this T-shaped cabin on the grounds of Appomattox Manor as his Civil War headquarters from 1864 to 1865.

The kitchen and other original dependencies still stand at Appomattox Manor.

Period antiques fill the restored interiors of Appomattox Manor.

One of the home's original tables, a letter-writing chest, and other period pieces furnish
Appomattox Manor.

Weston Manor retains almost all of its original hand-carved woodwork, such as this fireplace surround in the dining room.

Built on a high bluff, Weston Manor overlooks the Appomattox River close to where it joins the James.

A polished mahogany handrail decorates the original staircase at Weston Manor.

A reconstructed eighteenth century–style windmill grinds grain on windy days at Flowerdew Hundred, the site of the first windmill in North America.

Canada geese fill the air at Flowerdew Hundred. This area also attracts bald eagles and many other species of migratory birds.

property in 1624, it was a thriving tobacco plantation, one of the most prosperous of the James River communities. A 1625 muster and census shows that a total of fifty-seven men, women, and children lived on the plantation in twelve dwellings and that there were three storehouses, four tobacco barns, and a windmill. Flowerdew's settlers had ample supplies of corn, peas, and fish and tended almost seventy head of cattle and hogs. The inventory also included six cannon along with guns, armor, and swords, suggesting that the settlers were well prepared to defend the plantation from attacks by Indians or pirates.

When Abraham died in 1628, he left the estate to his daughter, Elizabeth Stephens. Documents indicate that the plantation may have suffered a temporary decline in the 1630s. William Barker, a prosperous merchant and ship captain, purchased the property in 1639 and developed Flowerdew into a profitable and important administrative and mercantile center.

78

A staff archaeologist at Flowerdew Hundred shows some of the artifacts unearthed in a recent excavation at the plantation. A museum on the grounds exhibits artifacts found at Flowerdew dating from 9000 B.C. to the Civil War period.

Through the centuries, Flowerdew Hundred was divided into smaller tracts. The plantation still produces substantial crops of corn, peanuts, and soybeans. Although none of the early plantation buildings remains at the site, a farmer plowing a field in 1971 found the stone foundation of one of the original structures. Since then, carefully planned archaeological excavations have revealed a complex of early seventeenth-century houses, including a forty-one-foot by twenty-four-foot stone foundation that was possibly the home of a high-ranking settler. The excavations and historical records indicate that as early as 1620, the colonists had built a manor house and at least eleven other buildings and had enclosed the community with a four-thousand-foot-long palisade. Remains of an eighteenth-century Georgian-style house have also been found, along with a storage pit filled with discarded eighteenth-century household items.

Archaeologists continue to dig into the secrets of the past at this historic plantation that was home to Paleo-Indian hunters about twelve thousand years ago. More than sixty-five sites have been located, yielding thousands of artifacts dating from 9000 B.C. through the Civil War.

The plantation is open to the public daily except Mondays from April 1 through November 30. A working reproduction of an eighteenth-century windmill grinds grain at the site, and the Flowerdew Hundred Foundation provides tours, exhibits, and educational programs to help visitors relive five centuries of life along the James River.

Grinding stones lie near the windmill.

Smith's Fort.

Bacon's Castle.

Seven

Smith's Fort Plantation
and Bacon's Castle

CAPTAIN John Smith, in 1609, ordered a fort built on the south shore of the James River directly across from Jamestown as a refuge for the colonists in case the Indians attacked the main settlement. Originally named New Fort, the site eventually became known as Smith's Fort Plantation.

Powhatan, the powerful chief who was the leader of more than thirty Indian tribes along the James, York, and Rappahannock rivers, gave the rights to the land to John Rolfe in 1614, when John married the chief's daughter Pocahontas. In 1616, John took Pocahontas to England, where their son Thomas was born. Pocahontas died at Gravesend, England, in 1617, and John died in 1622. Thomas inherited Smith's Fort Plantation and came to Virginia in 1635 to claim it.

Thomas Warren, who owned the adjoining land, bought the plantation in 1643. Warren built a home that was called the Fifty Foot House, a brick structure that measured fifty feet in length. Although this building has disappeared, its location on the plantation has been determined.

The existing manor house is a 1760s high-style, mid-Georgian, two-story structure, which was probably built by a descendant of Thomas Gray, who owned adjoining property. Many different families lived in the house and farmed the 350 acres of plantation land during the nineteenth century. The Association for the Preservation of Virginia Antiquities acquired the property in 1933, and John D. Rockefeller beautifully restored the house in 1935 when he was restoring and reconstructing nearby Colonial Williamsburg.

Costumed docents lead tours through the home, which is filled with authentic furnishings and fine woodwork. The Garden Club of Virginia maintains the grounds, including an English-style garden at the back of the house. The manor house, the grounds, and the site of New Fort are open to the public from mid-April through September.

At Bacon's Castle, just east of Smith's Fort Plantation, unsolved mysteries and the unique, well-documented seventeenth-century mansion standing on its original grounds are a historian's delight. Since 1973 the Association for the Preservation of Virginia Antiquities has sponsored research and archaeological excavations to unlock the secrets of this estate. The information that the association has uncovered has answered some questions and raised others about the man who built the imposing home and life at the estate during the seventeenth, eighteenth, and nineteenth centuries.

Documents record that a wealthy immigrant named Arthur Allen patented the land for the estate on March 14, 1650. Allen had come to Virginia in the early 1640s, but where he came from, why he came to Virginia, and how he obtained his wealth remain mysteries. It is possible that Arthur Allen might have been Arthur Guelph, a prince of the German

Buttered brickwork surrounds the front door
of the house at Smith's Fort Plantation.

Overlapping wood shingles form the roof
at Smith's Fort.

Ornate hand-carving decorates the dining room
chairs at Smith's Fort.

82

Two original wood cupboards flank the dining
room fireplace at Smith's Fort.

House of Hanover who allegedly had murdered his brother over the love of a highborn English lady and had fled first to England and then to Virginia.

Accounts indicate that Allen was a merchant-planter and that he served as a justice of the peace for the Surry County Court. It was not until 1665 that Allen built the high Jacobean–style brick mansion at his estate. At a time when most Virginians were building one-story houses, Allen chose to build a two-story castlelike structure in the shape of a cross, with a porch tower in the center of the front of the house and a stair tower in the center of the back. Triple chimneys, which are clustered at either end of the building and turned at an angle, accent the graceful curves of the Flemish gables and add to the medieval feeling of the house. Allen was fifty-seven years old when he built the mansion, a fact that has raised questions of why he built such an elaborate home in the Virginia wilderness so late in his life. Allen died just four years later, leaving the estate to his son, Major Arthur Allen II.

Major Allen, who served as the surveyor for the Colony of Virginia and as a justice of the peace of the Surry County Court, was a firm supporter of William Berkeley, the governor of Jamestown. The major was with the governor in September 1676 when Nathaniel Bacon burned Jamestown as part of his rebellion against Berkeley's government. About seventy of Bacon's followers broke into the major's mansion during his absence and used it as a stronghold for three months during the rebellion. Bacon's rebels plundered the estate, killing the livestock for food, trampling the crops, and ransacking the house. When British marines arrived at the estate in late December 1676, the rebels fled, stealing whatever they could carry. Major Allen returned to his estate and repaired the mansion, which came to be known as Bacon's Castle. The major died in 1710, leaving the estate to his wife and seven children. Eventually his son Arthur Allen III inherited the property.

Little is known about this Allen except that he was born about 1689 and, like his father and grandfather, served as a justice of the peace for the Surry County Court. It was his marriage to Elizabeth Bray that had the greatest effect on Bacon's Castle, for Elizabeth was an astute, intelligent, strong-willed woman who skillfully ruled the estate for the next sixty-three years. Eighteenth-century inventories of the estate indicate that Elizabeth refurnished the mansion. Closets, partitions, new window openings, raised-panel woodwork, and other renovations were also made to the home during this time. Elizabeth outlived Arthur Allen, two later husbands, and all of her children. When she died in 1774, she left Bacon's Castle to her grandson, Allan Cocke.

Like his forefathers, Cocke served as a justice of the peace and became the chief justice of the Surry County Court. He also was a member of the House of Burgesses and helped write the first constitution for the Commonwealth of Virginia. During the American Revolution, he was an active patriot and performed many military duties. Cocke died in 1780, leaving the estate to his son Benjamin Allen Cocke, when he came of age.

Benjamin inherited Bacon's Castle in 1794, but died five years later. In the next twelve years, ownership of the estate changed hands within the family seven times, until Benjamin's sister Ann and her husband, Richard Herbert Cocke, received the property.

Richard worked the plantation extensively. Historical documents record that in 1815 Richard operated a mill and an icehouse at the estate and used Bacon's Castle as a supply center for his stagecoach line, which ran between Portsmouth and Petersburg three times a week. By 1830, Richard had contracted to carry mail between the two cities. A successful entrepreneur, Richard was a very wealthy man when he died in 1833. Upon the death of his wife, Ann, five years later, Richard's granddaughter Indiana Allen Henley became mistress of Bacon's Castle.

This 400-year-old bed was brought
to Smith's Fort from England.

86   The original section of Bacon's Castle, on the left, forms a cross. The Neoclassical wing and the two-story connecting section date to the mid-nineteenth century.

Indiana and her husband, Dr. Robert Emmet Robinson, lived at the estate for about a year. During that time, Dr. Robinson wrote sonnets and poems on the windowpanes of the mansion proclaiming his love for his "Indy." When the Robinsons moved to Petersburg in 1839, they mortgaged the plantation. Indy died in 1841, and the mortgage on the estate was foreclosed in 1843. Thomas O'Sullivan bought Bacon's Castle when it was auctioned and sold it to John Henry Hankins in 1844.

Hankins was a planter, and he made Bacon's Castle into a profitable working plantation. He did not plant tobacco, but rather raised a variety of grain and garden crops. Under Hankins's management, the estate prospered, producing corn, wheat, oats, hay, cotton, sweet potatoes, white potatoes, peas, honey, beeswax, butter, and wool. By 1859, Hankins had purchased additional land for the estate and had renovated and remodeled the mansion, adding the large Neoclassical structure attached to the original house by a narrow two-story connector.

Hankins's daughter Virginia Wilson Hankins, known as Ginna, was strikingly beautiful and well educated. She captured the attention and heart of young Georgia poet Sidney Lanier, who was stationed at nearby Boykins Bluff on the James River during the Civil War. Lanier and his brother Clifford frequently visited Bacon's Castle, where Sidney and Ginna spent hours walking, riding horses, and sharing poetry. After the war ended, Lanier asked Ginna to marry him but she refused because her mother, who had died the day of Robert E. Lee's surrender, had left Ginna to care for her grief-stricken father and six young brothers and a baby sister. Even though Lanier later married, he and Ginna continued to correspond for the rest of his life.

Like the other James River plantations, Bacon's Castle faced the problems of loss of manpower and insurmountable debts in the years following the Civil War. Financially strapped, John Hankins mortgaged the estate shortly before his death in 1870. Unable to raise the money to pay the mortgage, Ginna and her brothers sold Bacon's Castle to the mortgage holder, Edwin White, who died soon after he moved into the mansion.

William Allen Warren bought the estate in 1880 and sold it to his son, Charles William Warren, in 1909. When Charles died in 1931, he left Bacon's Castle to his son, Walker Pegram Warren, who had been born in the mansion. Walker and his wife, Violet Norwood Lawson, used Bacon's Castle as a second home. The Warrens had no children, and following their deaths as a result of an automobile accident, the Association for the Preservation of Virginia Antiquities purchased the mansion, forty acres of the plantation, and a "mule named Kit" from the Warrens' estate in 1973.

Since that time, the association has worked to research, restore, and interpret Bacon's Castle. The mansion had suffered extensive termite and water damage through the centuries, and the association has made carefully planned repairs to stabilize and secure the structure without destroying the original craftsmanship of this National and State Historic Landmark.

Systematic archaeological excavations of the grounds surrounding the mansion have revealed a wealth of information about the original dependencies and landscaping of the property. The discovery of the circa 1680 formal garden next to the house is a particularly important find. Diggings have revealed the seventeenth-century grid-plan garden, with eighteenth- and nineteenth-century gardens above it, providing insights into the crops grown and how the inhabitants of Bacon's Castle used the garden area during the last three centuries.

This toy tool set from Victorian years is one of many historical exhibits provided by the Association for the Preservation of Virginia Antiquities at Bacon's Castle.

A spinning wheel and basket of cotton and other furnishings in this room reflect seventeenth-century life at Bacon's Castle.

The plantation smokehouse and other dependencies stand near the mansion at Bacon's Castle. This lock guarded the hams and other smoked meats.

Furnishings in this downstairs room depict the mansion as it might have looked in the eighteenth century.

Rather than remove all of the eighteenth- and nineteenth-century changes and try to return the entire mansion to its original 1665 appearance, the association has developed a plan to restore individual rooms in the home to the time period indicated by their surviving architectural elements. The "Over the Chamber" room on the second floor reflects the mansion's late-seventeenth-century plain interiors, with exposed beams of oak, whitewashed plaster covering the brickwork, and no baseboards, chair rails, or other decorative woodwork. The furnishings for this room are based on the 1711 room-by-room inventory of the house.

"The Hall," the east room on the first floor, has been restored to represent Bacon's Castle as it appeared in the eighteenth century. This room served as the main living and dining area for the inhabitants of the house during this period, and the association has furnished the room according to the 1755 house inventory.

Research and restoration work on Bacon's Castle continue as ongoing projects of the Association for the Preservation of Virginia Antiquities. The association opened the house and grounds to the public in 1974 and provides archaeological and architectural exhibits, a slide show, and guided tours to help visitors explore three centuries of America's history at this intriguing estate.

Brandon.

92

Chippokes Plantation.

Eight

Brandon Plantation and
Chippokes Plantation

A SPIRITED Englishman named John Martin came to Virginia with the first group of Jamestown settlers in 1607. After the terrible Starving Time of the winter of 1609, all of the settlers except Martin voted to go home to England. Determined that the settlement must not be abandoned, he was delighted that Lord Delaware, the new governor, arrived soon, bringing desperately needed supplies and more people to revitalize the community.

The sole surviving member of the original Jamestown Council, Martin repeatedly argued with Lord Delaware, however, and within a few months, the governor banished him from Jamestown. In the summer of 1610, he took a group of his followers and established a new community on the south shore of the James about five miles upstream from Jamestown. Martin's determination and hard work paid off, and instead of perishing, as the governor and others expected, his settlement prospered, producing profitable amounts of tobacco, potash, sturgeon, caviar, and other products that were shipped to England and sold.

In 1616–17, Martin received a grant for seven thousand acres and a charter for his settlement, known as Brandon Plantation. At his own expense, Martin built houses and transported people from England to his community, which was completely independent from Jamestown. The 1622 massacre caused the settlers temporarily to abandon the plantation. Even though the community was resettled, a raging fire completely destroyed the houses and outbuildings in the late 1620s. The losses at his plantation and his lack of success in collecting debts owed to him left Martin in financial ruin. He died, almost a pauper, in 1632 and was buried in an unmarked grave at Brandon.

Five years later, the three owners of the ship *Merchant's Hope* purchased the estate. John Sadler, Richard Quiney, and William Barber rebuilt the houses and dependencies, arranged for new settlers to come to the plantation, and restored Brandon as a profitable agricultural and commercial center. The heirs of the three owners successfully farmed the plantation until 1720 when they sold it to Nathaniel Harrison, the son of Benjamin Harrison II.

Although there were two four-room, 1-1/2-story brick houses on the property, Nathaniel did not live at Brandon. His son, Nathaniel Harrison II, was the first family member to move to the estate, and his friend Thomas Jefferson designed the estate's existing Palladian-style mansion. Jefferson suggested erecting a two-story center building between the two perfectly aligned existing buildings, expanding them to a full two stories and connecting them to the new center unit as wings of one building.

93

A pineapple finial, the colonial symbol of hospitality, sits atop the roof of the center structure. Hand-planed heart-pine paneling lines the walls of the mansion's formal rooms, and a triple arch, which is supported by columns topped with Greek-style capitals, spans the wide entrance hall.

Like so many of the homes along the James, Brandon bears the scars of at least two wars. During the Revolutionary War a British ship on the river fired at Brandon, leaving marks of the shelling on the house but doing no structural damage. During the Civil War, Union troops fired at the mansion and occupied the estate, using some of the paneling in the living room for firewood.

In 1926 the Daniel family bought the estate, and Congressman Robert V. Daniel and his family have made the mansion at Brandon their home for a number of years. A sweeping manicured lawn and beautiful gardens fill the three-hundred-foot area between the house and the river. Giant hardwoods, mature English yew trees, old-fashioned shrubs, and ancient pecan trees emphasize the age of the estate. A gnarled mulberry tree, planted more than three centuries ago, stands as a reminder of the attempts by the early colonists to establish a silk industry in America. Two huge cucumber trees mark the approach to the garden, which is protected by a double row of English boxwoods and stately tulip poplars.

One of America's oldest working plantations, Brandon still produces substantial crops of corn, soybeans, wheat, and barley and supports a beef herd and a commercial hog-raising operation. The grounds are open to the public daily, with the mansion open for tours only during Historic Garden Week each spring and at other times by appointment.

Downriver from Brandon is another working plantation first cultivated in the seventeenth century, Chippokes Plantation, established by Captain William Powell about 1618. Powell, who served as commander of the fort at Jamestown, patented 750 acres for his settlement and named it after Choupouke, a friendly Indian chief. Ironically, Chickahominy Indians killed Powell in 1623. His son, George, inherited the property and leased 300 acres of it to Stephen Webb, who built a house that was to remain part of the estate. When George died without heirs in 1643, the property reverted to the Crown of England.

Sir William Berkeley, then governor of Jamestown, gained control of the estate. After his death, his widow married Colonel A. Phillip Ludwell, and the couple moved into the Webb-Powell house at Chippokes. Later the Ludwell family moved back to their mansion near Jamestown, leaving Chippokes in the hands of overseers.

The plantation remained in the Ludwell family for four generations, during which the house at Chippokes was left to deteriorate. Ownership of the property changed hands many times, and at least two other homes were erected at the estate. One, a late-eighteenth-century house which now stands vacant, may have been built near or even on the foundation of the seventeenth-century Webb-Powell home. The other, the Greek Revival manor house and its dependencies, dates to 1854.

Mr. and Mrs. Victor Stewart purchased Chippokes at an auction in 1918 and set about to restore the home and grounds. Mrs. Stewart became interested in the history of the plantation and devoted years to researching and compiling information about the property and its inhabitants. In 1967, after her husband's death, she donated Chippokes Plantation to the Commonwealth of Virginia so that it could be preserved and developed for the benefit of others.

Playful statuary hides among the flowers and shrubs in Brandon's gardens.

Brandon's formal gardens lead to the edge of the James.

Authentic details and furnishings in the
kitchen and other dependencies make
Chippokes a living-history center.

The carriage house at Chippokes Plantation displays antique carriages and harnesses.

Now operated and managed as a state park, the grounds and furnished manor house are open to the public. Farmed continuously since 1621, Chippokes is still a working plantation as well as an educational and recreational center. The visitors center provides exhibits and audiovisual programs about Chippokes and other settlements along the James River. Interpretive programs range from nature walks to guided tours of the various plantation buildings. The park also offers hiking and bicycling trails and an automobile tour road. A swimming pool complex adds a modern touch to this historic site.

A gleaming silver service set displayed in the parlor indicates the opulent life-style enjoyed in centuries past at Chippokes.

98

Carter's Grove.

Nine

Wolstenholme Towne Site
and Carter's Grove

WHILE searching for remains of eighteenth-century dependencies at Carter's Grove plantation in the 1970s, Colonial Williamsburg resident archaeologist Ivor Noël Hume found a face-covering helmet from a suit of armor and other remnants of Wolstenholme, a fortified town that was built about 1620, wiped out by the Indians in 1622, and left forgotten for 350 years. This discovery sparked intense curiosity, resulting in a number of carefully planned excavations at the site that have revealed fascinating insights into daily life in this short-lived settlement.

Wolstenholme Towne served as the administrative center for Martin's Hundred, a large plantation patented by a group of British adventurers in 1618. Although the first shipload of 220 settlers left England for Virginia in the fall of 1618, for some unknown reason the plantation was not developed until 1620, when the settlers began constructing a fort on the land located about seven miles downriver from Jamestown. The Indians struck fast and hard at Wolstenholme in the Massacre of 1622, killing or carrying off at least half of the settlers and destroying the fort and homes. The village was not rebuilt, and the plantation, which by 1622 included 21,500 acres, was eventually divided into smaller, more manageable tracts and sold.

With the periodic flooding and tidal action of the James River, perhaps as much as half of Wolstenholme Towne has been lost to erosion. Since 1976, however, archaeologists have found evidence scattered over an area of more than fifty acres verifying the existence of the early-seventeenth-century community, which included farmsteads, storehouses, large and small dwellings, and one of the oldest British timber forts excavated in the New World. The fort, enclosing an area of about ten thousand square feet, could have held most, if not all, of Martin's Hundred's settlers. The fact that the settlers did not take refuge in the fort on the morning of the devastating massacre testifies to the overwhelming surprise element of the Indian attack.

The excavations have unearthed the graves of forty-eight settlers, some of them hastily buried after the massacre and others buried in coffins with gabled lids, similar to English coffins of the same period. Evidence of gable-lidded coffins, shards of delicate Chinese porcelain, and pieces of elaborately molded window leading suggest that the Wolstenholme Towne citizens made attempts to maintain their English life-style in the Virginia wilderness.

Partially reconstructed palisades, fences, and buildings now mark the outline of Wolstenholme. Visitors are invited to listen to audiotapes, look at displays and renderings of what the village may have looked like, and walk through the remains of one of America's first towns.

100   Tradition tells that Colonel Banastre Tarleton, a British cavalryman, slashed at the railing at Carter's Grove when he rode his horse up the stairway during the Revolutionary War.

According to local history, both George Washington and Thomas Jefferson were turned down in marriage in the "Refusal Room" at Carter's Grove.

Slave cabins are being reconstructed at Carter's Grove.

102   The grounds of Carter's
Grove sweep down to
the James.

The "front" door of Carter's Grove faces the James River.

Guests arriving via the carriage drive used this door knocker to announce their arrival.

This key and lock have secured Carter's Grove for more than two centuries.

On the crest of the hill overlooking Wolstenholme Towne and the James River stands the impressive eighteenth-century mansion that has been called the most beautiful house in America. The powerful and wealthy Robert "King" Carter purchased the property as a wedding gift for his daughter Elizabeth Carter Burwell. In accordance with King Carter's wishes, the estate was named Carter's Grove and became the property of Elizabeth's son, Carter Burwell, after her death.

It was Carter Burwell who constructed the handsome brick mansion. Begun in 1750 and taking five years to complete, the two-hundred-foot-long home is a masterpiece of Virginia architecture. The formal lines of the Georgian-style home reflect the cultured lifestyle of this influential colonial family. Attached dependencies flank the main house, and beautiful paneling and elegant hand-carved woodwork decorate the interior. According to tradition, the scars on the handrail of the staircase were made during the Revolutionary War by Colonel Banastre Tarleton, a British cavalryman who made Carter's Grove his headquarters and, according to legend, slashed the railing with his saber when he rode his horse up the stairs to wake his men sleeping in the second-floor bedrooms.

In the eighteenth and early nineteenth centuries, the Burwell family entertained often and lavishly at Carter's Grove. Many colonial leaders gathered at the home to discuss political and economic affairs, and lively social events brought together family members, friends, and notable guests. Romantic tradition says that the mansion's west drawing room was the scene of two famous refusals—Mary Cary refused George Washington's marriage proposal and Rebecca Burwell refused Thomas Jefferson's proposal—and that because of these two refusals, flowers placed in this room wilt overnight.

The lovely home remained in the Burwell family until it was sold in 1838, and ownership of the estate changed hands several times before Mr. and Mrs. Archibald M. McCrea purchased it in 1927. With the help of Richmond architect W. Duncan Lee, the McCreas carefully restored the home, which had suffered from years of neglect.

Now owned and maintained by Colonial Williamsburg, Carter's Grove is open to the public daily from March through November and during the Christmas season. The visitors center offers a film and exhibits about the plantation, and guides are available to answer questions and give tours of the mansion, which is beautifully furnished in the style of the Virginia landed gentry. Visitors are invited to explore the grounds of the plantation as well as the nearby site of Wolstenholme Towne.

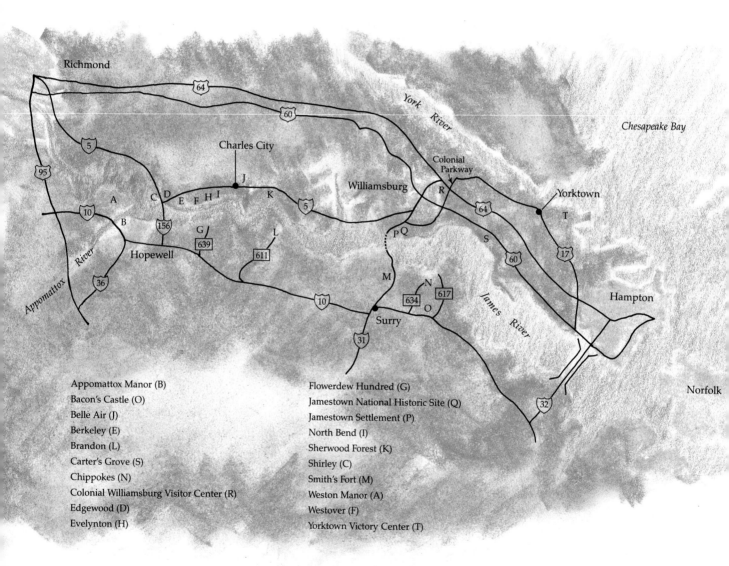

Richmond

64

60

York River

Chesapeake Bay

5

Charles City

95

J

Williamsburg

Colonial Parkway

Yorktown

A

C D

E F H I

K

5

R

64

T

10

156

G

L

P Q

S

B

639

611

60

17

Hopewell

Appomattox River

M

N

36

10

634

617

O

James River

Hampton

Surry

31

Norfolk

32

Appomattox Manor (B)
Bacon's Castle (O)
Belle Air (J)
Berkeley (E)
Brandon (L)
Carter's Grove (S)
Chippokes (N)
Colonial Williamsburg Visitor Center (R)
Edgewood (D)
Evelynton (H)

Flowerdew Hundred (G)
Jamestown National Historic Site (Q)
Jamestown Settlement (P)
North Bend (I)
Sherwood Forest (K)
Shirley (C)
Smith's Fort (M)
Weston Manor (A)
Westover (F)
Yorktown Victory Center (T)

Ten

Visiting the Plantations

VIRGINIA STATE 5 runs along the north shore of the James River between Richmond and Williamsburg, and State 10 runs along the south shore of the river through Hopewell toward Norfolk. The Benjamin Harrison Bridge (on State 156) crosses the James at Hopewell, and a toll ferry (on State 31) crosses the river near Jamestown.

Shirley Plantation is off State 5 halfway between Richmond and Williamsburg. Visitors can tour the eight-hundred-acre working plantation and visit the restored home, which is furnished with period pieces that have been handed down through the generations of the Hill-Carter family. The plantation is open daily except Christmas Day. For more information, contact Shirley Plantation, Charles City, Virginia 23030; (804) 795-2385.

Berkeley Hundred is off State 5 just east of Shirley Plantation, halfway between Richmond and Williamsburg. Visitors can tour the first floor of the historic mansion, which has been carefully restored and furnished with period pieces. Berkeley's ten acres of formal terraced boxwood gardens and lawn have also been restored and are open to the public. The plantation is open daily except Christmas Day. For more information, contact Berkeley, Charles City, Virginia 23030; (804) 829-6018. A re-enactment of the first American thanksgiving is held the first Sunday of each November. For more information, contact the Virginia Thanksgiving Festival, Box 5132, Richmond, Virginia 23220; (804) 747-1537.

Sherwood Forest is off State 5, 38 miles east of Richmond, 18 miles west of Williamsburg. The beautifully furnished home is open by appointment; the twelve-acre grounds, planted with some eighty varieties of trees, are open to the public daily. For more information, contact Sherwood Forest, Charles City, Virginia 23030; (804) 829-5377.

Belle Air Plantation is off State 5 just east of Charles City, halfway between Richmond and Williamsburg. The house and grounds, which include a formal herb garden near the outbuildings, are open to the public each spring during Virginia's Historic Garden Week and at other times for group tours by appointment. For more information, contact Belle Air Plantation, Route 1, Box 2, Charles City, Virginia 23030; (804) 829-2431.

Westover Plantation is off State 5 just east of Berkeley Hundred, about halfway between Richmond and Williamsburg. The grounds are open to the public daily, with the mansion open for tours only during Historic Garden Week each spring.

Evelynton Plantation is off State 5 just east of West-over Plantation, about halfway between Richmond and Williamsburg. The mansion and grounds are open daily, except for Thanksgiving, Christmas, and New Year's Day. For more information, contact Evelynton Plantation, Route 2, Box 145, Charles City, Virginia 23030; (804) 829-5068 or (804) 829-5075.

Weston Manor is off State 10 in Hopewell on the south shore of the James River. The estate is open for visitors during Historic Garden Week each spring and at other times by appointment. For more information, contact the Hopewell Tourism Bureau, Box 130, Hopewell, Virginia 23860; (804) 458-4829.

Appomattox Manor is off State 10 near Hopewell. The manor house and grounds are open daily. For more information, contact the Hopewell Tourism Bureau, Box 130, Hopewell, Virginia 23860; (804) 458-4829.

Flowerdew Hundred is off State 10 on Route 639 east of Hopewell. The grounds and visitors center are open daily except Mondays from April through November. For more information, contact Flowerdew Hundred Foundation, Hopewell, Virginia 23860; (804) 541-8897.

Brandon Plantation is off State 10 on Route 611 east of Flowerdew Hundred. The grounds are open daily, with the house open for visitors during Historic Garden Week each spring and at other times by appointment. For more information, call (804) 866-8416.

Smith's Fort Plantation is off State 10 on Route 31 across the James River from Jamestown. The house and grounds are open Wednesday through Saturday from April through September. For more information, call (804) 294-3872.

Bacon's Castle is off State 10 on Route 616, 6-1/2 miles east of Surry. The mansion and grounds are open daily from April through October. For more information, call (804) 357-5976.

Chippokes Plantation is off State 10 on Route 634 east of Surry. The mansion and grounds are open for prescheduled tours year-round. For more information, contact Chippokes Plantation State Park, Route 1, Box 213, Surry, Virginia 23883; (804) 294-3625.

Carter's Grove is off U.S. 60, 6 miles east of Williamsburg, and is connected to Colonial Williamsburg by a 6-1/2-mile-long protected road. The estate is open for visitors from March through November and during the Christmas season. For more information, contact Colonial Williamsburg, Box C, Williamsburg, Virginia 23187; (804) 229-1000.

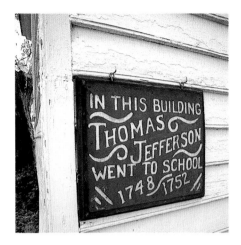

Tuckahoe Plantation, the boyhood home of Thomas Jefferson, is off River Road west of Richmond. The unusual H-shaped mansion, built in 1714 by the Randolph family, and the slave quarters and outbuildings form one of the most complete colonial plantation layouts still in existence. In 1935 the N. Addison Baker family saved the mansion from being dismantled and moved from the site for a museum display. Mr. and Mrs. Addison Baker Thompson currently live in the historic home, which they open to visitors by appointment. For more information, contact Tuckahoe Plantation, Box 369, River Road, Richmond, Virginia 23233; (804) 784-5736.

Edgewood Plantation is off State 5 close to Berkeley Hundred. It is open for visitors as a bed-and-breakfast inn and as a place for meetings and receptions. The mansion, with its fourteen rooms, ten fireplaces, five chimneys, and a freestanding, winding, three-story staircase, was built in 1849 by Spencer Rowland. During its colorful history, this Carpenter Gothic-style house has served as a restaurant, church, post office, telephone exchange, and nursing home. J. E. B. Stuart once stopped at this home for a cup of coffee, and the ghost of young Elizabeth "Lizzie" Rowland is said to haunt the estate. Lizzie, who etched her name in her upstairs bedroom window, died from a broken heart waiting for her lover to return from the Civil War. For more information, contact Edgewood Plantation, Route 2, Box 490, Charles City, Virginia 23030; (804) 829-2962.

North Bend Plantation, off State 5 on Route 619 just east of Westover, is also open as a bed-and-breakfast inn. The estate, which has been in the Copland family for three generations, is currently owned by the great-great-grandson of Edmund Ruffin. The home's heirloom furnishings trace the family history to the previous owners of Westover and Evelynton plantations. Mr. Copland still farms the 250 acres surrounding the Greek Revival house. For more information, contact North Bend Plantation, Route 1, Box 13A, Charles City, Virginia 23030; (804) 829-5176.

The Commonwealth of Virginia has re-created America's first permanent English settlement at **Jamestown Settlement** (formerly named Jamestown Festival Park), a living-history park close to the original site of Jamestown. The state-financed park has been extensively remodeled and includes the James Fort area, which depicts life in the settlement between 1610 and 1614; a re-creation of chief Powhatan's Indian village; reproductions of the three ships that carried the original settlers to Jamestown; and a museum complex. The park is open daily year-round, except Christmas and New Year's days. The park is off State 31 about 6 miles south of Williamsburg. For more information, contact Jamestown Settlement, Box JF, Williamsburg, Virginia 23187; (804) 229-1607.

The U.S. National Park Service and the Association for the Preservation of Virginia Antiquities maintain **Jamestown National Historic Site,** adjacent to Jamestown Settlement. The excavated foundations of the original buildings, exhibits, and recorded messages re-create the first permanent English community in this country. At the reconstructed glass factory, craftsmen demonstrate how the first glass was made in America. The site is open daily except Christmas Day. For more information, contact the Superintendent, Jamestown National Historic Site, Box 210, Yorktown, Virginia 23690; (804) 898-3400.

Northeast of Jamestown is **Yorktown Victory Center,** where exhibits, audiovisual programs, and a military encampment depict the major events of the American Revolution. Open daily except Christmas and New Year's days, the park is 12 miles east of Williamsburg off State 238 at the Colonial Parkway. For more information, contact Yorktown Victory Center, Box 1976, Yorktown, Virginia 23690; (804) 887-1776.

Colonial Williamsburg, which was the capital of Virginia from 1699 to 1780, offers over five hundred craft shops, taverns, public buildings, and residences that have been restored to their eighteenth-century appearance. Costumed guides relate the history of the buildings and the townspeople. The restored area is open year-round. For more information, contact Colonial Williamsburg, Box C, Williamsburg, Virginia 23187; (804) 229-1000.

Several riverboat companies offer cruises that provide narrated tours of the James River area. The riverboat trips allow visitors to see the front facades of the historic plantation mansions and to approach the estates as travelers in centuries past approached them. For more information, contact Richmond-on-the-James at (804) 780-0107, *Annabel Lee* at (804) 222-5700, *Pristine Mistress* at (804) 932-3075, James River Experience at (804) 323-0062, Harbor Cruises at 1-800-552-1533, or Charter Cruises at (804) 932-3075.

Index

Library of Congress
Cataloging-in-Publication Data

Roberts, Bruce, 1930–
    Plantation homes of the James River / Bruce Roberts ; with
editorial assistance from Elizabeth Kedash.
        p.   cm.
    ISBN 0-8078-1879-8. — ISBN 0-8078-4278-8 (pbk.)
    1. Plantations—Virginia—James River Region. 2. Architecture.
Colonial—Virginia—James River Region. 3. Architecture,
Modern—19th century—Virginia—James River Region. I. Kedash,
Elizabeth. II. Title.
NA7235.V52J356   1990
728.8'09755'4—dc20
                                        89-39204
                                        CIP